PETER SWINNERTON.
FM. 848 LANCS. F.B.

STEPHEN CHARLES

For my Mum and Dad, the most loving and caring parents anyone could wish for. Thank you for everything.

1. Getting there.
2. Pranks.
3. The big jobs.
4. Real life.
5. Trying to carry on.
6. The wilderness years.
7. All change. Part one.
8. All change. Part two.
9. Anxiety.
10. Fire safety.
11. The retained.
12. Bonfire night.
13. Battle of the sexes.

Foreword.

My first book, "Blood, Soot and Tears", although it covered a wide spectrum of events and subjects, was a concise summary my career in the London Fire Brigade. When it was published at the end of 2020, it was very well received, but the general consensus was that I should have written more. So, I set about writing this book to fill in some of the gaps but, once I started writing, it seemed to create a mind of its own and lead me from one subject to the next, each chapter developing in to something I didn't intend to write. The result has been a deeply personal account of my life in the Brigade. It is not just about station life and incidents, although there is plenty of that kind of content, it also delves into my personal struggles and how they affected my career.

I found myself trying to get across that, no matter what job you do, everyone has personal struggles that they are doing their best to deal with at the same time. When members of the public ask for help, whether from the Fire Brigade, Ambulance service, Police, Hospital staff, their GP, etc, they expect to be helped; and rightly so. They expect their problem or crisis to become top priority and to end with a satisfactory outcome. Again, quite right, so they should. But what is never considered are the personal problems and issues that the people who are helping them are dealing with at the same time. They don't know if we are going through a divorce, bereavement, bankruptcy, domestic abuse, or any of the many other problems that people go through every day. They don't consider what you may be struggling with, to them, you are there to solve their problems and that's it. So we do. We put our own issues aside and help other people with theirs.

There are going to be elements within the Fire Service that will be deeply unhappy with some of what I've written. So be it, I don't really care if I'm honest. This is my account of things and my opinion based on first-hand experience, as influenced by real events. I've opened my heart and laid my soul bare. Hopefully, I've put a few ghosts to rest in the process.

CHAPTER 1.

Getting there

After I applied to join the London Fire Brigade, while waiting to see if my application would be successful, I took a job with East London Buses as a driver. I hated it so much that, as soon as I could, I applied for a different job for the same company and ended up in the press and PR department. A big part of my job was dealing with and processing complaints from the general public. Passengers, motorists, pedestrians, even people who lived in houses that were on bus routes, they complained about anything and everything. I was very busy and very bored, but thoughts of what might lie ahead kept my mind occupied and got me through each day. Almost every morning, whilst waiting for my bus to work, I'd see fire engines driving to emergency calls, on the bell, (blue lights and two tones), and used to envy those on board. I craved the excitement that they must have felt. I would look into the rear cab and see the firemen getting rigged in their firegear and, sometimes, breathing apparatus sets en route to whatever they'd been called to. At the time, I didn't understand the significance of whether there was one, or two fire engines going on the shout. I didn't know why the crews sometimes pulled on hi-vis jerkins, either. What I did know was, I wanted to be where they were, doing what they were doing. Little did I know that, one day, I'd be serving at the very same station that they'd tipped out of and, in due course, I would be riding up front in charge of one of those fire engines. But, for now, it was just a pipe dream. Every evening, from my flat window, I would see the blue lights of the fire engines from my local station as they sped along the A13, a very busy road that goes into the heart of London, from Essex. It seemed like they were always on the go and, if I was lucky enough to get a job as a fireman, that's they kind of station I wanted to be posted to. There was something about seeing those lights and hearing the two tones and sirens that really used to spark my imagination. There I was, living a pretty mundane life, doing a boring job, or settled in my flat for the night watching TV, while these firemen were out at all hours, doing all sorts of wonderful and exciting things. I never thought too much about where or what they were going to, I just felt envious of the buzz that they must have been getting from their journey there.

My first taste of that would come at Southwark training centre on the day that I passed out as a fireman. We'd been using and learning about the fire engines, every single day for 6 months, but we never got to travel on them, or put the two tones on. Part of our passing out parade was to do a drill in front of our families. To make the drill more authentic, we were assigned two trainers to be our drivers, who drove us a little way from the training centre and then put the 'blues and twos' on for the short ride back, through the famous arch and into the drill yard. Suddenly, it all felt very real. The thing I remember, more than anything else, was the noise. It was incredible. The engines in those old Dennis and Dodge appliances were very loud. The two tones in the Dennis were worked by an air compressor in roof of the front cab, which damaged the ears of many drivers and Officers over the years. The modern sirens that were fitted to the Dodge weren't limited like they are today and really screamed at you inside the cab, especially if the windows were open, as they invariably were. The other thing that struck me was how heavy and lumbering these machines were. The drivers had to really fight with them to keep them going in the right direction. It still impresses me to this day how our LFB drivers used to throw these big lorries, carrying a very heavy load of water and equipment, around through the busy and narrow streets of London. I also discovered that day, that as practical as these appliances were for firefighting, they definitely weren't built for comfort!

Once I'd left Southwark Training Centre, I contacted the watch that I been assigned to serve with at my first station. It was tradition that the new bloke would meet the watch before their first day on duty and to take them cakes. I arranged to meet them on the second night duty of their tour. After the introductions were done, the governor, (Station Officer), asked if I'd like to ride with them if they had any shouts while I was there. I didn't need asking twice! Someone made a pot of tea and we all sat chatting and asking each other questions, getting to know a bit about each other. After about half an hour, the bells went down. It was all so new and exciting; I hadn't even heard the fire call bells from inside a fire station before. Calmly and orderly, everyone made towards the pole house and, one by one, slid down the pole into the appliance bay. My first lesson learnt, was to get off the mat at the bottom of the pole quickly! As my feet hit the round padded mat, I heard the screech of hands gripping the pole and looked up to see a fireman who had stopped himself halfway down to avoid landing on top of me. Even though these men were calm and unflustered, they moved quickly, hence why they could tip out two fire appliances within 60 seconds, or less, of the bells going down. Before I could even get to the Pump, the engines of both machines had roared into life and the bay doors were open, exposing the busy high Street outside. I had just had to grab a set of firegear that one of the previous watch had left out, as my own hadn't yet been delivered to the station from training centre, and do my best to get rigged whilst en route. The firegear was way too big for me. The boots were falling off my feet and the tunic and crotch of the leggings were hanging around my knees. Obviously, this gave the Pumps crew a good laugh at my expense, but I didn't care; I was going on my first shout. We had been called to smoke issuing, which means that someone has seen smoke coming from a structure and made the 999 call. As we got nearer to the address, I could smell smoke and started to get excited, thinking we had a job. But the bloke sitting on my left turned and said to me, "It's a paladin alight, you can tell by the sweet, sickly smell of the smoke. Dirty nappies have a smell of their own when they're alight. By the way, I'm Frank, but you can call me God", and started laughing. He was my Leading fireman and ended up being a huge influence on me throughout my career. As the Pump came to a halt at the bottom of the tower block we'd been called to, he got off and waved the Pump Ladder away. They weren't needed and drove off without stopping. They made me put the fire out and my first shout was under my belt. It was amazing to me at the time; speeding along the busy roads, with blue lights on and sirens screaming, switching to the wrong side of the road when necessary and going through red traffic lights. Once fire engines pull out of the station on a fire call, they very rarely stop until they get to the address. It was everything I thought it would be and more, because I was now part of it. After all the time it had taken to go through the application and selection process, then training, I'd finally reached the front line.

Riding as a passenger on the back of a fire engine on an emergency call, was one of the things that I thought might be a bit un-nerving before I went to a fire station. The reality was, it was the exact opposite. It was exciting and I loved it. A real 'buzz', as one driver described it to me. I was never interested in becoming a brigade driver because the driver never got to wear BA and go into a job, which was my passion. Instead, they'd be operating the pump, sending messages or looking after the BA entry control board. All extremely important jobs, but not what I was interesting in doing. To me, the buzz was all about donning BA and going inside buildings to search for casualties and fighting fires. One day, one of our drivers said to me, "That buzz that you feel when you go into a job, well us drivers get that buzz every time we drive out of the doors. Whether it's a bin alight or a person shut in lift, we get to drive through London on the bell and that in itself is a massive buzz". His words were very true and I appreciated them more as my career progressed. In the meantime, travelling to shouts as a passenger was fun. I enjoyed it and never felt nervous, until one day, when I heard through the RT radio speakers, those words that change the game totally. "Foxtrot 281, foxtrot 282, foxtrot 322, we are receiving multiple calls to this address. Persons believed to be involved". That's when the fun isn't funny anymore. Up until now, I had been impressed with our drivers and how they got from the station to the address, seemingly, without using the brakes. The first time I heard that persons reported message from the back of the pump ladder, I was to be impressed a whole lot more. The atmosphere on the appliance changed and I could physically feel everyone suddenly switch on. No more chit chat, no more laughing, no more banter. The cab went silent and the driver pushed the throttle pedal to the floor; and that's where it stayed. For the first time, I was actually concerned about my safety on the back of a fire engine. I was riding the PL. (pump ladder), and was rigging in BA, (breathing apparatus), en route, as the PL's crew did for all fire calls. As our driver threw the machine around like a rally driver, through the Saturday afternoon East London traffic, I was being chucked around the rear cab like a rag doll. (I later learned to rig with one hand while holding onto something solid with the other and, also, to look through the front windscreen to read the traffic and try to anticipate the driver's next move). As we neared the fire, we could see the pall of thick black smoke in the direction of our destination. That's the other thing that I was always impressed me with our drivers, their topography knowledge. We received this call Via RT, (radio telephony), while we were out on the fireground doing outside duties, (ie, shopping), but when we were called, the drivers, who always stayed with the machines, knew exactly where to go and knew the quickest route there. We all got there safely and what happened at that fire will be described in a subsequent chapter.

Being driven to emergency calls invoked various levels of excitement, danger, fear, humour, frustration and even anger; sometimes, all mixed together. I'm going to try to describe some of them as best I can. My first ride on a persons reported shout was pretty hairy, but we used to have one driver at my first station who had earned himself the nick name, Shunter. He used to drive to every shout like it was persons reported, regardless of what it was. He was a very skilful driver, everyone agreed, but he was mad. His one speed was flat out and every shout he drove me to was a white knuckle ride. I swear he could squeeze a fire engine through gaps in traffic that weren't there, without slowing down. It was like Moses parting the waves, cars used to go in all directions to get out of his way, some even mounted the pavement. Of course, he had the odd biff now and then, where he'd take a door mirror off a car, but he never had any serious accidents as far as I'm aware. The worst he did while driving me was to take the complete rear bumper off of a Ford Mondeo. But these incidents only happened because he possessed the skill to go for those impossible gaps that none of the other drivers attempted, unless they were driving to a persons reported fire of course. One night, he pulled off the impossible. Our pair, (Pump and Pump Ladder), were on the way to a shout late at night and Shunter was driving the Pump; the Ladder was about 40 yards in front of us. As the Pump Ladder passed a busy underground station, I saw a drunk stagger towards the road and, even though the blue lights and sirens were on, he seemed oblivious to the danger and almost stepped in front of it. He stopped himself just in time and escaped death by inches, only to step directly into the path of the Pump following behind. Shunter had nowhere to go. The man was in the road right front of us, too close for brakes to do any good. I braced myself and half closed my eyes, anticipating the inevitable impact. But it never came. I felt the machine lurch, opened my eyes and looked in the door mirror of the appliance to see the drunk continuing on his stagger to the other side of the road. To this day, I don't know how Shunter missed him, but like I say, he was a very skilful driver. This was one instance where things could have gone wrong, but didn't. There were many more over the years.

Another near miss came one day when my leading fireman, Frank, or God as he liked to be known, decided he was going to drive us to a shout instead of riding in front as the Officer in charge. He used to be a driver before he was promoted and wanted to keep his hand in. I suspect he also wanted to show us what an excellent driver he was. There was a big grass fire in progress on Wanstead Flats, which had tied up a lot of appliances, so we were providing fire cover over a much larger area than normal. The incident we'd been called to was a couple of stations grounds away, so it was going to be a long ride. Frank didn't waste any time in showing us what he could do and put his foot down. I remember thinking how confident he seemed to be, especially after not driving for a long time. Our regular driver, who had taken the leading fireman's front passenger seat, began to look very edgy and glanced over at Frank every few seconds. He had picked up on something that I knew nothing about at the time. All I knew, was that we were going faster and faster. Frank had become what they call 'bell happy'. As he hadn't driven for a while, the excitement and adrenalin had taken over and he was becoming mesmerised by the two tones. He was getting reckless and I started to get nervous, along with my mate on the back with me. Our driver was trying to tell him to slow down, but Frank just laughed. We were approaching a red light at a junction that we had to go through to cross Leytonstone High Road, which has a huge camber in places. We were going so fast, that he would never stopped for the red light if he'd had to, but he didn't even slow down. The front of the fire engine dipped sharply as we hit the bottom of the camber, then it launched itself skywards as we hit the top. I was lifted out of my seat as we came back down, but I swear the front wheels had become airborne because when we landed, we lurched sideways and ended up heading straight for a shop front on the corner. I thought that was our lot and braced for impact. But as the machine bounced again, we lurched the other way and ended up missing the shop and going in the intended direction! It weaved a bit for about 30 yards as Frank fought to regain control and miss the cars that were parked on both sides of the road, but we'd had a lucky escape. In true fireman fashion, once we'd got through the swearing and cursing, we all cracked up in fits of laughter. Looking back, one of the funniest things was the "FUUUUUUCK", that was shouted in unison by all four of us as we crossed the high road. When we got to the address, Frank just got off and said to our driver, "You can drive back, this driving lark is boring".

Another ride that could have been disastrous, but ended up being funny, happened when I was riding in charge of the Pump at my second station. We had a fireman who was detached onto our watch for a while. He got to like it and wanted to stay, so he reluctantly agreed to do the driving course that our Station manager insisted he do, if he wanted to remain on the watch. He passed his HGV test and the emergency driving course with the police and then he was let loose with a fire engine. Obviously, it was all new to him, so he was a bit nervous and cautious. In fact, he was so cautious that it was embarrassing, going along the road with blue lights and sirens on, with cyclists and motorists trying to overtake us. He didn't want to be a driver and he wasn't cut out for it. Not everyone is. He earned himself the nick name, Miss Daisy, because he was so slow. I used to get frustrated with him at times, but sympathised at the same time; although he never knew, because I was always moaning at him and telling to hurry up. One wet and rainy night, we got called to something or other and Miss Daisy was driving. I was riding in front as the officer in charge. The road conditions were terrible, with surface water and spray making driving difficult. But, for some reason, still unknown to me, he decided to put his foot down. Maybe there was football on TV and he wanted to get back to watch it, who knows? Either way, I was impressed with his new found confidence. He had a serious, determined look on his face. At the end of the high road, there was a one way system, which started with a very sharp left hand bend. In the middle of the one way system, was a cinema and a few shops on a big island. It was actually called, The Island, if I remember correctly. So, even though we were getting closer to the island, we hadn't started to slow down. I had been telling Miss daisy to hurry up for months, so I was reluctant to tell him to slow down now, even though I thought were approaching the sharp bend way too fast for the conditions. At the very last second, thankfully before I lost my bottle and yelled at him to slow down, he yanked the steering wheel hard to the left, in an attempt to take the left hand bend. Of course, nothing happened. The front tyres lost traction and we continued in a straight line, on a collision course with the island. I saw the metal railings and solid building coming at me and instinctively pulled my legs up to my chest and turned to face the rear cab, which was my intended escape route. I glanced over at Wilson and he had done the same. He had lifted his legs up and let go of the steering wheel, preparing for impact. Then, suddenly, the front tyres gripped the wet road surface again and slewed us round to the left, just avoiding the railings. I think the offside wheel actually hit the kerb on the way round. It all happened within a few seconds, then we both very quickly regained our composure; me, because I didn't want to appear scared and him because he needed to take control of the vehicle again; and carried on. I turned and looked at him and the only thing I could think of saying was, "Fucking hell, Wilson". He responded by saying, with a dead pan expression, "What? I did exactly as I was taught on my driving course. Come off the throttle, don't fight the wheel and let it come out of the skid". I, along with the two firemen on the back, burst into laughter and called him all the names under the sun. To this day, he still swears he was in control, when the reality is, he was trying to get into the rear cab before me.

You would be surprised at how other motorists react when they see and hear a fire engine approaching on the bell. Some simply panic, disengage their brain and do some of the most stupid things imaginable. Stamping on the brake pedal right in front of us seemed to be a favourite among the local population at one station I worked at. They would be oblivious to us approaching, even though we were in a big red lorry, with fluorescent yellow stripes down the sides, blue lights flashing and sirens screaming, until they happened to glance in the rear view mirror. Then, terror would overcome them and they'd perform a very impressive emergency stop, for reasons only known to them. This would cause our drivers to swerve in order avoid them, often onto the wrong side of the road, but sometimes they would choose a spot alongside an oblice or traffic island before hitting the brakes, which left our drivers nowhere to go. A ten ton fire engine, travelling at speed, isn't something you want bearing down on you. Thankfully, the fire engines brakes work very well, but the sharp stop didn't do anything for the crew in the back, who would be launched forward into the bulkhead. (We were supposed to wear seat belts, but no one ever did. You can't get rigged in fire gear or BA whilst wearing a seat belt). We developed a sixth sense when on shouts and almost knew what the driver in front was going to do, before they did. If was riding up front alongside the driver, I'd put my feet up on the dashboard and brace myself, if I was riding on the back, I'd use the bulkhead. The ideal thing would be for motorists to carry on driving until they come to a place where we could safely pass them, before pulling over to the kerb and stopping. But no, for a lot of people, that wasn't exciting enough. I've seen them mounting the pavement without even slowing down and, once or twice, even pull onto other peoples' driveways. Every now and then, we'd have a motorist try to outrun us, speeding ahead, jumping red traffic lights and all sorts. But the ones who annoyed us the most were those who used to tailgate us in order to get a clear run through the traffic. They couldn't see what was in front of us, so had no idea what our drivers might have to do next. Tailgating an emergency vehicle is such a dangerous and stupid thing to do.

I have to admit; I did shout and swear at many a motorist on the way to shouts. I even, on occasions, gave some interesting hand signals. But, as well as the frustration we experienced every time we went out the doors, there were plenty of funny occurrences, too. One such event happened around 7.30 am on the way to an AFA, (automatic fire alarm actuating), at a local Hospital; our pair, Pump and pump ladder, had been mobilised. The weather had been horrendous and we'd been up all night attending flood calls. A lot of roads were flooded and as we sped down the high road, I saw a huge puddle that covered the whole of our side of the road. Then I noticed a man walking out of a newsagent carrying his morning newspaper. From the pump behind, I could see what was about to happen. The pump ladder couldn't avoid the puddle, it had nowhere to go. The tidal wave created by a big vehicle driving through a foot of water, at speed, was something to behold. It covered the man from head to toe, with some force. As the water ran off of him, I saw him standing, arms outstretched and open mouthed, soggy newspaper in hand. But, just like the drunk outside the station years earlier, he had failed to notice the big red fire engine with flashing blue lights and sirens. He also failed to notice the equally bright and noisy one that was following it. He saw us at the last second and I'll never forget the look of impending doom on his face as we ploughed through the puddle and gave him a second drenching. As we continued, I looked in the door mirror and saw him throw his ruined newspaper to the ground. I've been splashed by cars going through little puddles in the past and it's not nice, but this was a different level. As tired and grumpy as we all were, after a night out on flood calls, we roared with laughter and our spirits were immediately lifted by this poor chap's misfortune. It still gets talked about to this day.

One day, we were joined by a driver who had been transferred to us from another station. His reputation had preceded him, as it always does in the Brigade. We were told that he was trouble and a bit of a loose cannon. I always take people as I find them and, when he arrived, I was surprised that he had such a bad reputation. He was a nice bloke and extremely funny. He had me in stitches many times with his very dry sense of humour. But, he was a character and always sailed close to the wind with certain Officers. As far as I was concerned, he was a good fireman, too. He was lazy on the station, but I went into a few fires with him in BA, (breathing apparatus), and he didn't put a foot wrong. However, he was a terrible driver. You never knew what you were going to get with him, from one shout to the next. He'd either drive like he was out for a Sunday afternoon drive with his granny, or he'd be driving foot to the floor and reckless. One night, we were ordered to standby at another station to provide fire cover, which is what used to happen if a neighbouring station had a job that they'd be tied up on for a few hours. There was no rush and no urgency but, for some reason, Dave decided to put his foot to the floor and keep it there. I was sitting alongside him and knew we were approaching a very sharp right hand bend. I kept expecting him to start coming off the throttle, but he didn't. At the last second, I shouted at him and he yanked the steering wheel round to the right. The fire engine went up onto two wheels but, somehow, made it around the bend. Right then, I knew something had to be done, or he could end up injuring or killing someone; so the next morning, I went to see our Officer in charge. "Mick, you're going to have to speak to Dave about his driving. It's very erratic. He nearly killed us last night". Mick said he'd have a word and called Dave to his office. I went upstairs to the TV room. About five minutes later, Dave walked into the TV room and sat down with a puzzled look on his face. "Steve, Mick just called me into his office and told me that I'm an erotic driver". Then I saw the grin breaking out on his face and we both burst out laughing. He was a funny bloke.

You never know when the bells would go down. Sometimes you could be on the way to the toilet when they dropped and you'd go out bursting for a pee. The incident, whatever it was, would take your mind off it, but the ride back to the station would be agony. We had one driver who would take great delight in driving back very slowly, going over every pot hole and drain cover, if he knew your bladder was about to burst. More than once, I had to threaten to piss on him if he didn't hurry up and get me back to the station quickly. The upside of his sadistic tendencies was, he used to get travel sick if he had to ride the back of the fire engine, so we all had opportunities to get our own back. As a junior officer and occasional officer in charge, I used to get to designate the runners and riders for every shift. On the rare occasions that we had a spare driver, I'd make sadistic Ken ride on the back and designate Miss Daisy as our driver. Ken always used to moan about riding on the back, not because he didn't want to get his hands dirty; he was a very good fireman; but because he used to suffer terrible with his motion sickness. Miss daisy knew this and would throw the machine around more than usual if Ken was riding the back, all the time with his silly grin on his face.

Driving back to the station from shouts was also quite entertaining, sometimes. Unbeknown to me when I joined the fire brigade, a lot of women seemed to have a 'thing' about firemen. In my mind, their illusions far outshone the reality. But on more occasions than I care to remember, when driving back from shouts late at night, groups of young, attractive girls would flash their boobs or bums at us as we passed them, tottering off home from their nights out clubbing. Forget all the flash and expensive cars, the best motor for attracting a girl's attention, by far, is definitely a fire engine. Just the same as all the top designer labels came a very poor second to the cheap fire brigade uniform we wore when we did entertainment licence visits in clubs and pubs, which were usually planned for Friday and Saturday nights. It wasn't always women that caught our eye, though. One event that is etched in my memory happened just a few months before I retired. We had been called to a large fire on a neighbouring station's fire ground. We had worked hard for hours on end, throughout the night, and we were all knackered when we left the scene of the fire. Driving back in the early hours of the morning, the roads were empty so we were heading back to the station at a fair rate of knots, in the hope we'd be able to catch up on a couple of hours sleep. I could hardly keep my eyes open when, suddenly, I was shocked out of my semi slumber by my driver, Pat, shouting, "Hedgehog, Hedgehog, Hedgehog!!", as he took quite severe evasive action. As my eyes focused, I saw a hedgehog walking across the road in front of us. Everyone loves a Hedgehog, so I was pleased that this one didn't end up as just another spiky pizza.

CHAPTER 2.

Pranks

This is a very sensitive subject to write about, but I feel it is necessary to give people a better understanding of the way the fire service worked - and should continue to work, in my opinion. It was always taken as read, that when you joined a firefighting watch as a junior buck, you would be tested; and rightly so. Pranks, jokes and wind ups are the stuff of fire brigade lore. It is what builds the unbreakable trust, loyalty and faith which you must possess if you are to be able to do the job effectively and become a valuable part of the watch. I've heard stories of abuse and bullying that took place on some watches. Whether there is any truth in them, I don't know; but what I do know, is that I never witnessed anything like that during my 25 years in the Brigade. What I did witness, (and was subjected to, along with every other 'buck' in the Brigade), however, was practical jokes, mickey taking and high jinks which have, on occasions, been mistaken for abuse and bullying. Usually, by those looking in from the outside, rather than those who were actually part of the fun. Before going any further, I'll try to set the scene. When you are selected to become a recruit firefighter, you've already beaten many thousands of other people who also applied, but were unsuccessful. Your confidence is high. Then you spend six months in training school in a close knit squad of 12 other recruits. There could be ten squads there at any one time, all at various stages of their training. You soon find out that you are the bottom of the ladder, so to speak. Watching more advance squads pitching ladders, pumping water by various methods, wearing Breathing Apparatus for drills, while you are just trying to get used to moving in your heavy and cumbersome firegear and learning how to roll out lengths of hose, your new found confidence takes a knock. As squads finish their training and pass out, brand new squads come in and you move up the ladder, provided you continue to reach the stringent standards and pass all your tests. Gradually, you climb the ladder until you are the squad that is preparing for final tests and exams. At this stage, you have more knowledge and experience than all the other recruits on site and your confidence is sky high again. When you pass out in front of your family and get posted to a real watch on a real fire station, you think that you know everything and can do anything. You believe that this is the most highly trained you will ever be. What you don't realise at the time is, you have zero experience in being a real firefighter. Everything up to this point has been make believe. Then you enter the real world, where it isn't make believe any more and people could die if you don't get it right. Experienced watches have seen many new recruits who arrive on the station thinking that they know everything. They have a duty to bring you up to speed but, first, they have to drag you back down to earth so that you actually start listening to them. In my eyes, this could be achieved in two ways. One way is to allow the recruit to do their own thing, make mistakes and give them a dressing down every time they do. This, in my opinion, is counter - productive because it demoralises the recruit, destroys any confidence they may have had and alienates them from the watch, therefore, isolating them. The traditional and preferred method is to involve the recruit in a whole host of practical jokes, mickey taking and high jinks. This lets the recruit know, in the nicest possible way, that he is back at the bottom of the ladder again but, instead of isolating him from the watch, it allows him to bond with them. When I was the buck and messed up, given the choice between formal action or a soaking from the watch, I would choose the soaking every time, not that I was given the choice. To some people, one person being soaked by a several others could be construed as abuse or bullying, especially in today's touchy feely culture.

I didn't have to wait long before the practical jokes started when I joined my first watch. On my first Sunday daytime shift, while the rest of us were lined up for roll call in our firegear, one bloke was stood in in his undress uniform. The roll was called and we were each given our riding positions on whatever appliance we would be riding for the shift. Each appliance had a designated hydrant location man. His job would be to look in the hydrant location book; which gave the exact location of every hydrant on the stations ground; en route to fire calls and to find the nearest one to the address that we'd been called to. On arrival, it was his job to take the stand pipe, key and bar and set into the hydrant, in case we needed it. In training school, every hydrant in the yard had a false spindle fitted. (A false spindle was a tapered piece of cast iron that fitted over the small square spindle that modern hydrants were made with, so that our old tapered hydrant keys would fit whatever type of hydrant we had to use, old, which had tapered spindles, or modern.), but out on the fireground, it was rare to find one fitted as they'd all been stolen. Therefore, we used to carry a few false spindles on the appliances. I was detailed as hydrant location man on the pump and given 'my' false spindle by the previous buck, who ceremoniously took it out of his tunic pocket and handed it to me. I was the new buck and hydrant location man, now, and had to carry it in my tunic pocket. It was a horrible, heavy and cumbersome piece of equipment, but the reasoning was that, if I found I needed a false spindle to set in to the nearest hydrant, it would be a waste of valuable time and energy to run back to the fire engine to get one. It all sounded feasible. So, although I wasn't thrilled with this new practice that we hadn't needed at training school, it made sense, I was the new boy and I didn't question it.

When it came to the bloke dressed in his Sunday best, he was detailed church duty. I was told that it was his turn to attend the service at the church next door. Apparently, it was an age old tradition that, every Sunday, someone from the on duty watch at this station would attend church. It seemed a bit unusual, but who was I to question it? Maybe they were superstitious, or it had something to do with keeping them safe? I had no idea, but it seemed feasible; after all, I knew the Brigade had its own Padre who visited stations from time to time. Then, with roll call done, it was, "Red watch, red watch 'shun. To your duties, fall out.", and we got on with testing our BA sets and doing all our usual checks, while the bloke in his undress uniform disappeared. When we went upstairs afterwards, for a cup of tea, I was told that next Sunday, it would be my turn to go to church. Again, I wasn't thrilled, but who was I to argue? So when the next Sunday dayshift arrived, as everyone else was getting rigged in firegear ready for roll call, I was told to get into my undress uniform, ready for church. After roll call, I was sent upstairs to get a cup of tea, while the others went about their routines. When I got to the mess, the weekend cook said to me, "Aah, is it your turn to go to church today love?" The others gradually filtered upstairs and took their seats at the mess table, then the governor came up and told me to start making my way next door, as they'd be starting soon and I didn't want to walk in mid service. So off I went, all shiny and new, not knowing a thing about what was to come. When I got inside the church, the Vicar welcomed me and said was always nice when they got visitors from the fire station next door. This was reassuring, but the Vicar was a black man dressed in a white suit, shirt and tie, rather than the robes that I'd seen Vicars wear in the past. I went in and took a seat among all the friendly smiling faces. Then it dawned on me. I was the only white person in the church and I was in my undress uniform while everyone else was dressed for the occasion. The men wore smart suits and the women wore bright, colourful, flowery dresses. When the Vicar started his sermon, I realised that this was an evangelical church, unlike anything I'd ever seen before. The atmosphere was one of sheer joy and happiness. I'll never forget the sound of them all singing together in harmony, swaying and clapping. It was quite beautiful. I stayed for what I thought was an acceptable hour, then, during the break, I made my excuses and left. When I got back to the station, I was greeted with laughter and mickey taking, of course. One of the old hands on the watch then looked up at the watchroom clock on the wall and said, "An hour. That's not bad. When Trigger on the white watch went a few months ago, he stayed for the full four hours!" It was an elaborate prank, but they got me, fair and square. We all had a good laugh about it and the bonding had begun.

I soon found out that all of the pranks were very elaborate and planned with precision. As a new boy, you have no choice but to believe what you're being told. After all, this was a whole new world and I didn't have a clue about station life. Everything was strange and new. Even the different noises that I heard, that prompted different reactions from the watch. The station telephone had a sound of its own and there were two different tones, depending on whether the call was coming from inside or outside the brigade network. The tele-printer in the watchroom made beeping noise as messages came in, then, there were the bells signals that all meant something to everyone except me. The appliance dispatch lights, red for the pump ladder, green for the pump, told everyone who was going out the doors when the fire call bells went down. Whoever got to the bottom of the sliding pole first would look at the lights and shout up, "Pump only", or "Pair", to save the ladders crew from coming down if it was a pump only shout. The watchroom, or box, as it was known, in itself was very confusing. The designated man on duty in the watchroom, (duty man), had to take care of everything that came through our communication system during his shift 'in the box'. As I've said before, life on a fire station is, to the uninitiated, like life in a different world. So everything and anything is feasible, until you learn otherwise. On my first night, I was told I would have to sleep on my mattress on the floor of the watchroom with the duty man, so that I could see and learn what the duties were. Apart from everything else, the duty man sleeps in the watchroom at night to man the phones and tele printer. Also, to receive and acknowledge the call from control at 06.40 hrs, to wake station personnel, or call staff, as it was termed. The duty man then had 20 minutes to get washed, dressed and make a pot of tea for the watch, before the 07.00 hrs bells; which would be put down by control, like a shout, to make sure everyone was awake. The truth is, the duty man would rush to get ready and make the tea, then go to the watchroom to silence the bells and cancel the lights, (all station lights come on when the bells go down), so as not to wake the watch. I remember standing over the printer watching the second hand of the clock, so that I could cancel the bells and turn off the lights before they disturbed my mates, who had invariably been up most the night answering fire calls. The watch would then be given a much gentler awakening, by having a cup of tea placed by their bed and told it was time to get up. So, with so much to learn and remember, sleeping in the watchroom at night seemed like a sensible idea. Even though it was supposed to be another prank, it did me well. I learnt watchroom duties very quickly and was soon able to be duty man on my own. The duty man rides the pump ladder and the pump ladders crew get to rig in BA, (breathing apparatus), and go into any fires that were picked up. I was eager to get into real fires and to do the job I was trained to do, so learning watchroom duties quickly, meant I went into fires earlier than I might have, if my watch hadn't been so up front with the banter, pranks and the lighter side of the job.

However, although sleeping on the watchroom floor backfired on the watch and worked in my favour, the second half of the prank totally got me. About mid-evening, my leading fireman asked if I'd been issued with a mattress when I left training school. I obviously hadn't. He then started moaning about how I should have been, how things weren't how they used to be and that he'd order me one right now. He phoned the North East area staff office and put the order in. About an hour later, the inquiry bell rang to let us know that someone was at the front door downstairs. A few minutes later, I was called, via the station tannoy, to come down and sign for my new mattress. When I got downstairs, there was a divisional van parked up on the forecourt and a fireman I'd not seen before, with my leading fireman, in the watchroom; on the floor, was a new mattress, neatly rolled and tied up with the appropriate paper work and label attached. I was told that when I put my bedding away in the morning, to put the mattress in my locker but, not to worry, because after a few months, once I'd got to know everyone on the station, I'd probably be able to share a mattress with someone on another watch. That way, it wouldn't have to be put away every morning. It was, of course, as ridiculous as it sounded, but who was I to argue? This was my first night shift in a whole new, weird and wonderful world, so I did as I was told and the joke ran for a couple of tours before it died a death and the mattress became a spare for the station.

As I've said, the jokes and pranks pulled on the junior buck were planned carefully and quite elaborate. A lot of effort went into them. The next and, probably, last one that I was subjected to was my six monthly report. I knew my six monthly review was approaching, when I would be questioned and drilled by my station commander, to make sure I was making satisfactory progress. It was the half way mark in my years' probation period. The tour before my six monthly was due, (a tour was two day shifts and two night shifts, after which we'd have our days off), I was summoned to the office again by my sadistic leading fireman. "Before you go in front of the ADO, (assistant divisional officer), your watch officers have to write a report for him, so this is what we've written. Read it and sign it. I had been working hard for six months, getting to grips with station life and being useful on the fireground, so I was eager to see what impression I'd made on the watch and my officers. I took the report and started to read and, as I did, my heart dropped. It wasn't what I wanted, or expected. It was a scathing account of my first six months in the job. But the more I read, the more I suspected that this was just another wind up, so I turned the tables. I gave the report back to my Lfm, (leading fireman), and refused to sign it. I said, "If I'm as bad as you say I am in that report, I'm a liability and danger to myself and everyone else. In which case, I've got no right being here and might as well jack it in now". He looked at me and I saw he was struggling to keep a straight face, so I started laughing and he also burst into laughter. We re-read the report together, cracking up over each paragraph as it got worse and worse, then he said, "Well done. When I did Alf's last year, he said he agreed with some of my comments and signed his report!" Alf was the buck on the watch one year before me. When we went back up to the mess and the rest of the watch, it was poor old Alf who got all the stick because he'd actually signed his spoof six monthly report. Like I've said, there was no bullying involved, everyone went through it. No one was excluded.

It wasn't just on my watch, either, it was across the whole brigade. I remember at the start of one night shift on a hot summers' evening, we got a call from the next station down the line. They had a request for us. "Can you bring your pump over? Our new buck will be sitting on a chair on the forecourt, we've told him that there's a convoy of hazardous materials scheduled to pass the station, escorted by your pump, and to let us know when it appears so that we can take over the escort. He's been out there for an hour already, so can you pull up and give him a soaking for us?" Ten minutes later, we drove onto their forecourt, pulled off two hosereels and gave their buck a soaking. He ran away and the rest of his watch came out for a chat and a laugh with us. When the buck had changed into dry clothes, he joined us and laughed along with everyone else. We all knew he wasn't stupid, the plot was totally feasible. This prank, along with all the others, was just the start of becoming part of a very close knit team. Every buck went through similar scenarios, not because they were being singled out or anything like that; in fact, it was the opposite. It was all part of our welcome into the London Fire Brigade and all that came with it, ie, the need to laugh in the face of adversity, to shrug things off and just get on with it and to not take life too seriously.

Christmas was always taken very seriously in the LFB. As we spent so many Christmases away from our families, it was always a big deal among watches to make the best of it. Christmas dinner was always a special occasion on the station and all the stops were pulled out. The watch would rally round and help the mess manager to prepare a proper Christmas feast. There would be crackers and party hats, which everyone wore, and retired members of the watch would be invited to join us on this special day. There were also after dinner speeches. A tradition of old was that the junior buck would stand up and give the first speech, thanking the watch for all their help and for being so welcoming, etc. No one really listened to what was being said, because they were all waiting for the speech to end, so that they could pelt the buck with brussel sprouts and potatoes. But that was just the start of the festivities, because it would invariably lead to an all-out food fight among the watch, usually followed by a water fight. It was, strange as it may seem to the uninitiated, a real bonding session for the buck. To see all the watch having food thrown at them and being able to throw it at them, too, reinforced the knowledge that you weren't being singled out or bullied. It was explained to me, perfectly I think, by an old hand on my first watch. He said, "If you can take fire brigade banter and laugh it off, you can deal with anything you're likely to encounter out on the fireground. You're now part of a special club, where if you were injured with multiple wounds, we'd stick our fingers in the holes to stop your blood from pissing out".

The pranks never stopped when I completed my probation period, but it became a much more level playing field. Anyone and everyone was fair game. A few of my favourites were the ones which came as a sudden and total surprise to the victim. On a few occasions, the toes were cut out of socks during the night while the owner slept, clothes neatly piled next to his bed, ready for a quick getaway if the bells went down. It was hilarious when they did at some ungodly hour, seeing the bloke pull his socks right up to his thighs before realising that he'd been done. It lifted the spirits of the rest us and we'd still be chuckling as we pulled out of the station on the way to whatever the shout was. Another well-known one, which I never got to witness, unfortunately, was cutting a fireman's leggings off at the knees and folding them back over his boots. When the watch got rigged for roll call, there would be one fireman standing to attention in front of the Governor wearing fireboots and shorts with braces. I think the best and most elaborate 'wheeze' that I ever heard about was aimed at a Stn O at a neighbouring station. All four watches were in on it, including the officers, but the poor chap didn't have a clue. Someone decided to invent a new piece of kit which would be exclusively for Stn O's; no one else could be trusted with it. There was only one on the station, so it would have to handed over to the oncoming Officer in charge on roll call at change of watch. It was the continuous use night torch. The person who dreamed this one up had even gone to the bother of typing out an operation note for it, telling the white hats how and when it should be used. The Op note was handed to the oncoming officer in charge with the torch, which was just a bike torch. The heading on the Op note was "Continuous Use Night Torch. (C.U.N.T). The unfortunate Stn O relished in his new found importance for months, sometimes holding up the night torch and pointing at the rank markings on his shoulder and saying, "You want one of these, get some of these". It went on for so long that everyone just got fed up with it in the end and told him. Of course, he said he'd known all along.

CHAPTER 3.

The big jobs

I remember my first big job quite clearly. I had been at my first station a few months and had been lucky enough to have picked up several 'bread and butter' jobs. I'd worn BA in anger a few times and even been on a few four pump fires, but, for some reason, I yearned to go on a really big job. We'd been ordered to stand by at other stations while they attended big jobs, to provide fire cover on their grounds, but never been ordered onto the actual job itself. That changed on one warm summers' night, when I was riding the back of the pump. I was at a busy station, so no one ever went to bed much before 1.00 am, (yes, we had beds and used them!). Around 1.30 am, the bells went down and our pump was ordered to stand by at the next station down the line to provide fire cover. When we got there, as was standard practice, I signed on in the watchroom and we looked at the tele-printer roll to see what they had and to get a rough idea of how long we might be standing by there. They were on a six pump fire, Chicksand Street, on Whitechapel's ground. That meant they would be gone at least an hour, probably two, so we hunkered down as best we could to get some sleep. Half an hour later, the bells went down and we were ordered to stand by at another station a bit closer to Whitechapel. When we got there, we saw that the fire had gone to eight pumps, which meant it had got worse. Still, we all found somewhere to put our heads down to try to get some sleep, resigned to the fact that we'd be there for a good while now. We must have been there for an hour or so, because I'd managed to find a comfy spot on the floor and actually drop into a deep sleep. I was awakened by the bells going down and the lights flooding the station with fluorescent daylight. Into the watchroom again I went, where I met our driver, standing at the teleprinter in his underpants. He'd decided to sleep on the watchroom floor and as he tore the call slip from the printer, he said, "It's gone to 15 and we're going on it."

Being inexperienced and mad keen, I immediately felt excited and made my way to our pump with a spring in my step. A 15 pump fire, just up the road, and I was going on it! All sorts of images and thoughts went through my mind. Meanwhile, the rest of the crew were making themselves' busy, collecting their bedding and going for a piss before ambling to the pump. I couldn't understand their lack of urgency. We pulled out of the station on the bell, (blue lights and two tones), because it was an emergency call this time. We hadn't been called to stand by somewhere, or onto a relief; we had been called to a 15 pump fire as part of the attendance. Once we were on our way, the older hands said to me, "Don't get too excited, Steve, all you'll be doing is standing around for hours and probably won't get to do anything." This didn't make any sense to me at the time. There was a fire that someone had made up to 15 pumps – and we were needed – right?

We arrived at the RVP, (Rendezvous point), to an unbelievable scene, to me anyway. There were fire engines and other specialist appliances as far as I could see and the whole road was being lit up with blue lights. Even though we were parked some distance from the fire, the sky above me was glowing orange and there was a spectacular shower of bright burning embers falling from above us. I stood there open mouthed. I'd never seen anything like it. It was truly spectacular but, then, the first pangs of anxiety started to course through me. This was not play time any more, this was serious. As we walked towards the fire to report to the command unit, (CU), we were bumping into groups of friends and colleagues from other stations. There was much mickey taking, laughing and joking going on, even at this ungodly hour. As our leading firemen was booking us in attendance on the CU, the rest of us stood chatting to other crews; some who had been there for over an hour and still hadn't done anything yet. After about 10 minutes, the leading fireman came back and gave us the brief he'd been given by the senior officers on the Unit. We had to go back to our pump and don our BA sets, then report to BA entry control, which was close to the actual building that was alight. Up until now, we had been one or two streets away from it. As we got nearer to the scene of operations, we started to see the maze of red fire hoses that had been laid out in all directions, criss-crossing as they went in and out of various pumping appliances towards the fire. Stepping over it as we went, the noise of the fire began to overwhelm the noise of the pumps revving the closer we got to it. My first sight of the fire left me open mouthed and more than a little bit apprehensive. From memory, it was a big three or four story building on a corner and according to the messages we'd seen, it was used as a warehouse. Every window had burnt out and there were flames punching out horizontally, half way across the road from the ground and first floor ones, before rolling up the outside walls. Part of the roof had collapsed, along with most internal walls. Through the flames, which illuminated the inside of the building, we could see huge steel beams that had lost their strength and started to buckle and bend. The noise of the fire was incredible. It sounded like a furnace, literally roaring; the sound of walls falling and the creaking from the steel bending added to the scariness of it all.

The BA entry control point was positioned across and down the street a bit from the fire. There were about 6 other BA crews ready and standing by, waiting to be sent in. It seemed inconceivable to me that they would actually commit us into this fire, but that's what they had planned to do. The officer in charge of the Entry control point came over and gave us our brief. "Right lads, we've pulled everyone out for now, but we're just about to start committing crews again. When we do, you lot are the emergency team." Great, I thought, so we get to go in when the shit has already hit the fan! There were a few crews who had obviously been in earlier and been pulled out. Their helmets blackened by soot and grimy faces streaked with sweat. There was a bit of radio traffic that I could half hear over all the other noise, then, the Officer told us that they weren't committing any more BA crews into the building, but told us to keep our sets on and report to a senior officer around the other side of the building. When we got there, we met a Divisional Officer who was well known in the area and very well respected. He was what we called a fireman's fireman, ie, very experienced, sensible and fair. He told us to reposition some lengths of hose and to get two jets to work from the roof of an adjacent building, to fight the fire from the outside by aiming the jets through the burnt out windows. We were just happy that we were actually going to be doing something and, secretly, that we hadn't had to go inside the building. As I was dragging charged hose to where we wanted it, the Officer walked up to me and said, "See that big wall there? Well it's about to collapse and when it does; it's going to land right here. So keep a close eye on it and drag the hose a bit further away." Eventually, we started our sets, which were required due to the thick smoke all around us, and went to the roof to start aiming water onto the fire. Being new and inexperienced, I thought we would actually start putting the raging inferno out. Instead, I watched as my solid jet of water turned to steam as soon as it got anywhere near the fire. We could see several other crews on other roofs, all trying to do the same thing. It was futile, but at least it was safer than going inside the building; although, one of the firemen from anther station did manage to fall off the roof he was on and get injured.

We went back to that building the next night on a relief and I think there were still reliefs going on when we came back on duty four days later. That was my first taste of a really big job and, all things considered, it wasn't a bad introduction. Over the years, I attended many fires that were 10 pumps and above and quickly began to hate going on them. It wasn't because they were hard; it was because they always frustrated the hell out of me. As soon as a job was 'made up', (more appliances requested), a lot of things are set in motion. One being, for a four pump fire, an assistant divisional officer, (ADO), is ordered on with the additional appliances. Most of the time, this wasn't a problem. The ADO was usually paged from home at some ungodly hour and didn't really want to get involved when he got there. He'd just monitor the job until everything was under control and then go back home to bed. However, as the years rolled by, things changed a bit and we started to get some ADO's turn up that had probably been promoted above their own ability. These officers didn't really have the experience or confidence to leave the job in the capable hands of the station officer, nor to take over charge and take responsibility for it. So they'd often make the job up again, because a make pumps six message gets you a divisional officer, who then takes over from them. The thing is in the fire brigade, usually, the higher the rank, the less experience of actual firefighting the officer has had. We did have good experienced officers, of course, but they became few and far between as the brigade started to promote younger and younger people, based on what they call competence, rather than experience. An up and coming officer could 'prove' his competence by acting out scenarios at make believe incidents and table top exercises. It wasn't unusual to get very senior officers turn up at a big job, with a lot less experience and knowledge than the firemen doing the work. A lot of the time, these officers would try to run the job from the CU, as if it was another table top exercise. This would invariably result in confusion, delays, constantly changing plans and, luckily for NCP, a site for another car park in London as the building often burnt to the ground.

I was always pleased when we turned up at a big make up to see an old time, experienced senior officer in charge of things. They would walk around the job to see for themselves what was going on and would talk to the working crews, listening carefully to whatever bit of observations and advice they might offer. Then they would make decisions based on what they saw and heard in real time. Most of these officers knew almost everyone working on the ground, because they had spent a lot of years serving at local fire stations before going for promotion. The firemen knew and remembered them. If they had been good firemen, good junior officers and fair station officers, then become good senior officers, they were respected and we all used to trust them. For the firemen like me, who hadn't really bothered with promotion and spent all their careers on fire stations, it was usually first name terms between them and us because we'd known each other for years. Not so with most of the young upstarts with a lot of ambition and not a lot else. I'm convinced they believed that the rank markings on their shoulders possessed mystical powers which would instil knowledge and wisdom into them overnight. I attended so many big fires where the troops on the ground had arrived and started dealing with it, making good progress, only for senior officers to turn up and try to rearrange everything, reposition everyone and change tactics on a whim. It was like they couldn't grasp that the fire was happening in real time and every delay or pause in firefighting would result in it getting a stronger hold. I can't tell you how frustrating that is. When firemen are messed around too much, they stop using their own initiative and start following orders to the letter, even if they know it's all going to go tits up. As with anything in the fire brigade, this often presented an opportunity for some humour and fun. I remember when we were all given our own personal fireground radios. Until then, it was just junior officers and above who were issued with them. Now, suddenly, everyone on the fireground could be heard by everybody else. Sometimes, there would be confusion and little disagreements between senior officers, some of them quite tense, which was hilarious to hear when you can see the fire getting bigger because of their incompetence. When smart phones became must have items, you'd sometimes hear someone playing 'Entrance of the Gladiators', (the tune that became synonymous with clowns in the circus, despite its rich history and origins), over the airwaves from their phone. With so many fireground radios switched on, it could be heard all around the job. Everyone would be in hysterics, apart from the senior officers, of course. Big fires always meant lots of hanging around with little activity, so any humour was always welcome because it broke up the monotony.

Another thing that used to happen when the CU arrived, was the handing out of tabards to anyone who didn't make themselves scarce enough when various roles were allocated. There were tabards for such roles as Officer in charge, (OIC), safety officer, sector commander, facilitator, comms operator, entry control officer, monitoring officer, etc, etc. As a junior officer, I was a prime target for a tabard, so whenever I saw someone walking around with a handful of them to dish out, I'd walk off in the opposite direction. I preferred the freedom of being able to walk around the job to see if anything useful could be done, or checking with other working crews to see if they wanted a hand. Being given a tabard meant that you were rooted to the spot and constrained by the task you'd been given. Most of the time, the task was extremely boring. One exception that I remember was at an eight pump fire on Barking's ground. It was a big warehouse that covered quite an area and there were a couple of firefighting teams on each side. A senior officer that I knew and liked, had been given the job of facilitator, which meant he had to check on all the crews to see if there was anything they needed, like more hose, more jets, ground monitors, BA cylinders, etc. He already had his tabard on, so thinking that they'd already all been handed out, I felt safe and didn't bother trying to hide. Instead, I thought I'd walk around the building and find somewhere my crew and I could get stuck into the firefighting. Preferably, somewhere not too far from BA entry control, so that if they required more wearers to commit, we'd be on hand. My plans were shot to bits, however, when someone called me up on my fire ground radio and told me to report to the CU. At big jobs, all crews had to hand in nominal roll boards on arrival, so that those on the CU knew exactly who was there. The positive side of this was that if there was an evacuation, a collapse or a backdraft, they could carry out a proper roll call and quickly find out if anyone was missing. The down side was, they knew what rank everyone was and could allocate them jobs and tabards. I went to the CU, where I was told, "Go and find ADO Smith, he's got the facilitators tabard on. You're going to be his assistant, here's your tabard." Bollocks! I found the said officer and told him that I was now his assistant. He grinned from behind his big moustache and said, "OK, follow me." and took off on a tour of the fireground. As he walked, he turned and said, "My job is to find out what the crews need, your job is to arrange it for them." He was a good officer and well respected by all the blokes, but boy, could he walk fast! I struggled to keep up with him as he went from crew to crew, asking what they were doing and if there was anything they needed. I lost count of the laps we did of that building, but I was knackered by the time we got relieved and had big painful blisters on both feet. Still, it was better than being designated safety officer and being bored all night.

If there was one thing worse than being held back by senior officers at big jobs, which happened too often in my opinion, it was being held back by firemen. There was a certain type of fireman that, when given a tabard to wear, became overcome by their new found authority. Even if they were decent firemen or junior officers, the tabard would do something to them that changed their attitude. Personally, I think it was their inability to deal with the responsibility that had been bestowed on them. I saw this happen time after time, but one incident sticks out in my mind. One night, we were called to a six pump fire on the boarder of Essex and London. The address and map didn't give any indication that it was anything serious, but you never know until you get there and have a look. The fire was in the back of beyond and, when we arrived, we were briefed to take up position and become an intermediate pump in a water relay. A water relay is set up when the water supply is very poor and we a chain of pumping appliances, all plumbed into each other, are set up to boost the water pressure all the way to the fire. We were the third or fourth pump from the hydrant, so quite a way from the fire. Once we'd got positioned and all set up, there was very little to do. How boring! So, as usual, I decided to have a walk about to see what all the fuss was about. After all, we were in the arse end of nowhere and I couldn't see anything from where we were. The radio traffic was relatively quiet for a six pumper, too. I followed the line of fire engines, then the delivery hose lines from the fireground pump, until I came to the fire that was causing all the trouble. I couldn't quite believe what I was seeing. It was nothing more than a big hole in the ground, in the middle of a field, full up with the products of a bit of ground clearance; largely dead trees, branches, brush and undergrowth, along with a load of other wood, which was probably a demolished barn or something similar. It was well alight, but posed no threat to anyone or anything. It wasn't going anywhere, but it wasn't going out, either. From the edge of the fire, I could see that no one was actually fighting the fire effectively. A series of ground monitors had been positioned around the giant fire pit. Ground monitors are good because no one has to hold them and they can deliver a lot of water over quite a distance. Ideal if you're dealing with dangerous chemicals, cylinders or anything else that you don't want firefighters going too close to. The down side is, you can't see exactly where you're aiming the monitor and their effectiveness for firefighting is limited. They're alright for cooling things down, but you can't fight a fire effectively with them alone. It struck me that the only reason why this fire had gone to six, was the sheer amount of water that the monitors were demanding. A senior officer came over to me and told me to get my crew and position yet another ground monitor where I was standing. The pumps were already struggling to supply enough water, as it was and a water shuttle – where a fire engine drives away from the job, fills its tank and shuttles the water back to the fireground - had been set up to augment the water supply from a different water main some distance away. It was what we used to call, a 'cluster fuck'. I went back to our pump and told my crew to bring two lengths of 70mm hose each and a couple of branches, then we all set off back to the fire. We laid our hose out from where the shuttle pump was positioned, to the spot where they wanted to other monitor positioned. When the shuttle arrived back with a full tank of water, we plugged straight into it and our branches into the other end. Then we went to the edge of the hole, went halfway down the bank and started putting the fire out. It was only wood and it wasn't tightly compacted, so it started going out quite quickly once attacked directly. Happy days! At rubbish fires in the early hours of the morning, everyone just wants to get it done and get back to their station. Suddenly, a junior officer appeared and started trying to call us back. I knew him and he was a decent sort. A bit silly sometimes, but a nice bloke all the same. "You can't go down there, it's dangerous!" I looked at him and saw that he'd been given the safety officer's tabards to wear. "Oh right, who says so?" He pointed to his tabard and said, "Me. I'm safety officer." I ignored him and carried on, which made him a bit agitated. He came over and said, "No, really, you can't be down here. It's dangerous" "Why? What's dangerous about a big hole full of wood?" I asked, "Look, we're actually starting to put it out." He didn't have a valid argument and looked a bit embarrassed. He'd been given a job and given a tabard to wear, so he felt important and thought he had to do something to fulfil his role of safety officer, whether it needed doing or not. His parting shot was, "Well, you might fall over." I laughed, along with my crew, and promised him that we'd be very careful. Shortly afterwards, a senior officer came over to see what we were doing. He chatted briefly, saw the progress we were making and walked off. There was a bit or Radio chatter, then we noticed that the ground monitors were being knocked off and replaced with branches; then we saw other crews coming forward to attack the fire from all sides. After a few hours, the fire was out and we were told to knock off and make up. Fire ground speak for, get your stuff together and go home. As we were making up our hose, I stretched my back out and leant against a fire engine. I was knackered after holding the weight of charged 70mm hose for two hours. Just then, another senior officer came walking over; someone I knew very well and had worked with for years. "You OK mate?" he asked. "Yeah mate, I've been on a jet for the last two hours and my back is feeling it now." I said. He laughed and said, "You fucking love it, Steve, don't you. Hate everything else, but fucking love getting stuck in." We both laughed and went our separate ways. He was right, though. To me, at big jobs, it was black and white. I either wanted to get stuck in, or go home. Any time I was in charge of a crew, I'd have a look around and try to find us something useful to do. If there wasn't anything, or the job had been strangled by overzealous officers and their procedures, I'd always try to get us away at the earliest opportunity.

Something unusual happened one night at an 8 pump fire on a neighbouring stations ground. It was a carpet warehouse and it was well and truly ablaze, in fact, about half way there, we could see the sky glowing orange. When we arrived, it was still early days as we had only come from next door, as it were. Hose was still being run out all around the building, a water supply was being sorted out and there was still a good recce to be carried out. While the men sorted out the water, I took a walk around the building to see exactly what was involved and to gather as much information as I could, to pass on to the station officer in charge. I knew him from old and the first time I caught a glimpse of him, he was running up and down the length of the warehouse, shouting orders and instructions to no one in particular. He was in cabbage mode, head off, cabbage on, and seemed to want everything done at once. Immediately! At the same time! I tried to grab him as he ran past me, but he was gone. I don't think he even saw me. Just then, a cylinder exploded inside the warehouse. The shockwave opened up a big crack in the blockwork of the building. Everyone carried on doing what they were doing, but crouched a little bit lower, which was a natural reaction to the explosion, rather than a conscious one. Then we all looked around at each other and laughed. This was the jolt that the Stn O needed and he quickly regained his composure and actually did an OK job after that. A few more cylinder exploded, so it was decided that we couldn't enter and would just have to be content to stop the fire spreading to any other nearby units. A while later, the fire broke through the roof and, then, it was just a matter of time before the whole building collapsed. We repositioned all the hose and moved back to a safe distance, just aiming water into gaps in the walls as they appeared and putting cooling jets onto surrounding building. I was quite enjoying this job. The explosions had provided a bit of excitement and a talking point, plus, it was nice to see the job going from initial chaos, to a controlled firefighting operation. But things were about to get a bit more interesting. A member of the public, who had dodged the police cordon, approached me and asked what the chances of getting into his unit would be. "No chance mate. The flames from the fire are already licking the outside of your unit." He asked me to show him, so I took him round the other side to have a look. When he saw it, he looked mortified. "I've got to get in there! There's fifty grand in cash inside there. It's my life savings and I can't just let it burn." The poor bloke was almost in tears and I felt sorry for him. There was a policeman standing close by and he even pleaded with the copper to let him go inside. The policeman obviously refused. I took the bloke aside and said, "How about if me and my mate go in and get your cash out for you? I think I can wangle that, otherwise you're fucked mate." I asked him where the cash was, which he was reluctant to tell me, but after a few seconds thought said, "half of it is on top of the third roof truss on the left. The other half is in a false wall in the office, next to the door." I told him to give me the keys, then; me and my mate went and fetched an extension ladder and a big crow bar. I approached the copper and told him that we had to go inside the unit to check for fire spread and that the owner had kindly given me the keys to make our entry quick and easy. We'd be in and out in no time. He had no choice but to agree and stood aside. We unlocked the big doors and went inside, had a quick check for fire spread and closed them behind us, so that no one could see that we were in there. We didn't hang about and pitched the ladder to the top of the roof truss first. I went up and had a feel about with my hands. I came across a plastic bag, grabbed it and came back down the ladder. We then set about removing the false wall and found the second bag quite quickly. £50000 is a lot of money now, but back then it was a huge amount of money. I'd never seen so much cash and probably never will. We stuffed the bags down our leggings and made our way out. I nodded to the copper and said, "All looks good in there mate, so we've locked it up again." We didn't have to look too far for the owner; he was looking for us and almost pounced on us when we came into view. I took him to one side and handed over his life savings, which he stuffed into a Tesco carrier bag. Then, without even as much as a thank you, he walked off with it into the night. He didn't even offer us a drink! Ungrateful bastard! It was about then that I realised that, to the general public, all we are is their servants. We were public servants. What we did was expected and taken for granted. And I suppose that's how it should be, really.

Southwark training centre in the old days.

STEPHEN CHARLES

The famous archway into STC.

BA training with ther arch visible in the background. I'm in the centre.

WHEN THE BELLS GO DOWN

My first watch. I'm front row, second from the left.

Red watch book club. I'm third from right.

Me, second from the right, roof ladder training.

Frank O'mara and myself after ladder rescues. (B,S&T

CHAPTER 4.

Real Life

People often said to me, "I couldn't do your job and deal with all the stuff that you have to". But they never stopped to think about what else I might have had going on in my life which, a lot of the time, was harder for me to deal with than anything I experienced at work. Everyone has things to deal with in their private lives and it's all relative to that individual. What is terrible for one person might be a breeze to someone else – and vice versa. I have no doubt that work related stress, when added to personal problems, compounds and results in mental turmoil. If there's no release and no respite, at work or at home, it puts the individual under extreme pressure just to function. I make no apologies for taking a chapter to give examples taken from my own experiences, detailing how they affected me and my ability to function as an effective firefighter. I already knew a bit about stress, depression and anxiety before I joined the Brigade, due to everyday things like divorce, unemployment, etc. These are things that almost everyone experiences these days, so nothing out of the ordinary. I had served three years in the London fire brigade and thought I was cruising through life. I was married again, just bought a lovely house in rural Essex, had a good secure job which I loved and just found out that I was to become a Father, something I'd longed for as long as I can remember. I was a happy man. But little did I know that my life was to be turned upside down before my fourth year of service.

The pregnancy went like a dream. No morning sickness, no problems with any of the routine checks, everything was normal.

We decorated the small bedroom in neutral colours because we didn't know, or care, what sex the baby would be. As the months passed, we became more confident and started buying the essentials. Pram, cot, baby clothes, nappies, you name it, we bought it. We loved our visits to Mothercare and even bought little cuddly toys and a mobile for hanging above the cot. When the baby became very active, I used to put my hand on my wife's belly and talk to him or her. When she was in the bath, I used to get handfuls of water and let it drop on her big bump, to make our baby wriggle. It was an amazing time. On the day our baby was due, my wife started to experience some cramps, which she thought were mild contractions. It had been a text book pregnancy, so we thought there was a very good chance that the baby would come on the date we were given. My family had come to visit from London and, while they were there, my wife went to the loo and lost some blood, so that was another sign that things were moving. As it was our first, we phoned the hospital and were told it was normal, nothing to worry about, but come in if you want to. About half an hour later, she went to the loo again. This time, she thought her waters had broken, but there was more blood; a lot more blood. After another call to the hospital, we decided to grab the bag we had packed and go straight to the maternity ward. I felt nervous, but very excited at the thought of meeting my first child that day. My family decided to hang around at my house so they could be there, should the baby put in an early appearance.

We were taken straight into a delivery room and met the midwife who would be there with us throughout the birth. By now, my wife was in a lot of pain. The machine they had her hooked up with was showing strong and frequent contractions, but the midwife was confused because my wife hadn't even started dilating yet. We could all hear the baby's heartbeat on the monitor and were reassured that the baby wasn't in distress. But the pain had become unbearable for my wife. I started to worry that something wasn't right. Eventually, the midwife said she was going to call the consultant with the view of delivering the baby by caesarean section. I remember feeling a wave of relief come over me, because I knew that the pain and suffering would end soon. The midwife started to prepare my wife for theatre, then, the consultant came into the delivery room. He asked for a scanner but, before it was brought in, told the midwife to get her to theatre straight away and that he was going to scrub up. This was now going to be an emergency caesarean. A porter came in and my wife was whisked off with the midwife following. I was left in the delivery room on my own, wondering what on earth was going on. I was worried, but still confident that everything would be OK soon, because she was in good hands.

I thought I'd use the time I had on my hands to call my family and update them on what was happening. Everyone was pleased and excited that my baby would be with us very soon. I went back to the delivery room and waited and waited and waited. Hours passed and there wasn't any news, no one came. I walked outside into the lobby to ask if everything was alright, just as a porter rushed in with a loaded trolley, asking the receptionist where the blood had to go. I felt a twinge of apprehension, but was assured that someone would update me soon and to go back to the delivery room. I went back and sat down, still not knowing why it was all taking so long. Then I heard footsteps approaching along the corridor outside. It sounded like there were quite a few people coming, but I couldn't hear a baby crying. The door burst open and I was suddenly surrounded by a small group of people. The midwife, a few nurses, a doctor and someone else. Straight away, I realised that something was terribly wrong. My blood ran cold, it really did, but no one said anything. They all just stood, looking at me. I looked at everyone in turn, to try to get some sort of reaction, but all I got were looks back. So I blurted out, "Is someone going to tell me, then, or what?" Only then did the doctor speak up, at last. "The baby isn't making it", he said, then, I noticed that one of the nurses had started to cry. I knew then that my baby had died. Although I'd become completely numb by now,

I focused on my wife and asked if she was alright. "They're stitching her up now and then she'll be taken to recovery. Once she's there, we'll take you up to see her". This was all too much to take in and I felt I was living in a bad dream. How can one of the happiest days in my life, suddenly turn into the most tragic? I wanted to break down and cry, but I couldn't. It was just total disbelief and I half expected someone to come in and say there had been a mistake and that everything was alright, after all. Still, everyone was just looking at me. I eventually managed to squeeze some tears out, but I can't remember feeling anything. Then, the consultant came in, straight out of theatre. He was more upfront than the others had been and walked straight up to me. He sounded quite angry when he spoke. "You sit there crying, but you've still got your wife. You are lucky. She had lost so much blood and her womb was like an Aubergine. I had to massage it for twenty minutes to save it, so that you can have another baby. You are lucky to still have your wife. She had to have three blood transfusions and we almost lost her".

The rest of the day and night are a blur to me. I remember a few things happening, but have no idea of the timeline. It was like a terrible dream that I kept thinking I'd wake up from. There had to be a mistake, right? At some point, I was taken to the recovery room where my wife was just coming round from the anaesthetic. I sat by her side and took her hand. There were two nurses standing at the foot of the bed. She opened her eyes, very groggy, and the first words she spoke when she saw me were, "Where's the baby"? How do you deal with that? What do you say to the woman who has carried your baby for the last nine months, but then has nothing to hold and love at the end of it? Where do you find the strength to subject her to the news that had totally destroyed me, earlier? I squeezed her hand as best I could around the canula and whispered, "He didn't make it". She was barely conscious, but her eyes immediately welled up and she turned away from me. Then, with a puzzled look, she said, "But everything was alright". At this point I turned to the two nurses for some sort of support, but they were both crying their eyes out. I really can't remember anything else after that, until we got on the ward that she'd be staying in. She had a private room on the maternity ward. We were surrounded by new mums, happy dads and new born babies; but we had nothing but emptiness. They put us on a maternity ward, rather than put a couple who have just lost a baby, on a general ward. Afterwards, I discovered that the reasoning was, she had given birth, the same as all the other women on the ward, so why shouldn't she be on the maternity ward? When they asked if we wanted to see him, I didn't think I could. I didn't think I could cope with so much anguish, but my wife was adamant that she wanted to; and she was right. It was 100% the right thing to do, no matter how upsetting it would be.

When they brought him into the room, he was wrapped up and dressed like any other newborn baby would be. He had a little blue bonnet on and a little knitted cardigan under the baby blanket. The midwife handed him to my wife, who cradled him and held him close, trying to smile through her tears. That sight completely destroyed me. I didn't have to force the tears any more, they just came flooding out. I went to her side and held them both, then I picked him up in my own arms and sat down with him. As I wiped my tears away and my vision became clearer, I was struck by how perfect he was. All his tiny features were perfect, his little hands and fingers, his nose and lips. I felt overwhelming love for him and fully expected him to take a breath and start living now that Daddy had him. I gave him a kiss on the forehead and put him back in the little cot that they brought him in. As I did, my Mum, Dad and older sister came into the room, accompanied by another nurse. Again, it was all an emotional blur, but I can remember my Mum picking my baby boy up and rocking him as she held him close. My sister went straight to my wife and gave her a massive hug. No matter how I try to describe it, nothing can really capture the emotion and grief in that room. I began to feel guilty for inflicting all that upset on my wife and my family. I felt responsible for it, like I'd let everyone down because things didn't turn out OK. Most of all, I felt like I'd let my son down. When he really needed his Dad, I couldn't do anything to help him and I hated myself for it. I hated that he was dead, but I was still alive. It just wasn't fair.

The hospital gave me a bed on the ward, so that I could stay with my wife. I would go home for a while each day to bring things that we needed and we both left the hospital after 5 days. When we got back home, it was surreal. It was just how we'd left it on that fateful day. The pram was in the lounge, the moses basket was in our bedroom, the cot was in the baby's room, along with a bathing and changing trolley. A mobile hung above the cot and there were soft toys dotted about. There was a great big hole in our lives and we felt thoroughly cheated. Then there was the horrible business of going to register our baby's birth and death on the same day, which had to be done before we could start arranging the funeral. A vicar came to visit us at home after a few days, wanting to offer his sympathy and ask how we wanted the funeral to go. We both said we didn't want hymns or prayers, because any faith we might have had, had been severely dented. He understood and asked us to write something that he could read out during the service, instead; which we did. The day of the funeral arrived, along with my family, who came to my house so that we could travel to the cemetery together. We met my wife's family there. I was very surprised to see two members of my watch standing on their own outside the chapel. They actually reported for duty that morning, but managed to get special leave for the funeral and raced from London to Colchester on a motor bike. I walked over to them and held my hand out, but they pulled me in and both hugged me. I'll never forget that, as long as I live. Then, the car pulled up outside, but I didn't want to look at it. We all went in and took our seats. I turned to see a single undertaker walking along the aisle carrying a tiny white coffin in his arms. I, along with everyone else there, broke down in uncontrollable tears. All through the service, I just looked at the little coffin and longed to go and get my baby boy out of there. I wanted to take him home with me, but I couldn't. And then, it was all over.

CHAPTER 5.

Trying to carry on

Going back to work after losing my child was surreal. It almost felt like an out of body experience. I knew that I was seeing and talking to people, but it was like I was a spectator watching myself from a distance. I was deep inside my own head and everything else going on was on the outside. I felt numb and detached from everyone and everything. But I desperately tried to appear normal to the people around me, who themselves felt very awkward and struggled to appear normal to me. No one knew what to say to me and I didn't know what to say to them, so we all behaved as if nothing had happened. At the start of the watch when I went to take my firegear from its peg in the gear room, I almost couldn't touch it because it was exactly where I had hung it when I went off duty the last time before my life was turned upside down. I thought to myself, "When I hung this here, everything was alright. I don't want to take it off the peg because, if I leave it there, everything might still be alright." It was crazy, I know, but that's how my mind was working. I was still clutching at straws and thinking it was still all just a bad dream that I'd wake up from. On my first night shift, the same thing happened. I went to get my bedding out from my bedding locker and was abruptly reminded that when I last put it away, everything was alright. Everything else I did for the first time after my return to work was the same and slammed home the same thoughts and feelings. The only thing that didn't was the sound of the bells going down and turning out to emergency calls. These were the only times that I could totally forget about what had happened before and be focused on what I was doing. Those shouts were the only thing that brought some normality back to my life and gave my mind a rest. In the following weeks and tours of duty, I found myself alone with individual members of my watch and we'd have quiet chats about things that were avoided in front of others. It was as hard for them as it was for me, but, eventually, I'd managed to speak to all of my watch and the awkwardness gradually diminished. I was still fighting a battle inside, but I didn't feel so bad if I was caught gazing out of the mess window in silence. I now felt that my watch, my brothers, understood and were supporting me by giving me space and time to be alone with my thoughts.

Away from work, a massive hole had been left in our lives. Something, someone, who should have been there with us, wasn't; and it was very hard to bear. My wife and I felt we'd been cheated out of the life we wanted and decided to try for another baby at the earliest opportunity. A few months after I returned to work, we were blessed. I can't describe the joy we both felt when the pregnancy was confirmed. I didn't want to tell anyone too early, but due to the circumstances, losing a baby at full term, we were given a date for an elective caesarean at 38 weeks and knew exactly what day our baby would be born on. I contained my excitement at work because I didn't want to tempt fate or, bizarrely, let anyone down again. But that changed when the annual leave allocation for the following year came through at the station. As usual, we were only allowed to have two of the watch on leave at the same time, to maintain ridership numbers. My watch was a close knit watch and we always worked out the leave between us without the need for any lists or rotas, which was quite unusual. When they asked me if I had any preference of when I took my annual leave, I said I'd like a few weeks in August, if possible. Again, unusual because July and August were always given to those watch members with school age children, for the school summer holidays. No one said anything, but it was like the penny had dropped. "Are you doing anything special in August then, Steve?" A few were grinning, so I couldn't keep it secret any more. "Yes, my baby will be arriving on the fourth and I'd like to be there." I said, unable to contain the huge smile on my face. Their reaction was one of sheer, genuine joy. It was a special moment and made me feel even closer to my watch. They'd shared the tragedy with me, now they were sharing the joy. I didn't know then, but it would lead to a bitter sweet situation.

As the initial euphoria gradually decreased, anxiety took over. Fear of something going wrong gripped me, along with the feeling that I had before about not being able to do anything if it did. We had moved away from London a few years previous and were living in a village just outside Colchester, Essex. My station was a great station, but the traffic in that part of London made the journey long and miserable. Going to work wasn't as bad as coming home, because I could leave early, but it would take me two and a half hours to get home after my day shifts; longer if there was an accident on the A12. That worried me a lot. If I got a phone call saying something had or was going wrong, I'd be useless. My anxiety ate away at me while I was trying to battle through the traffic and only started to ease when I was on the home stretch of the A12. I spoke to my watch about putting in for a transfer to a station that was only 8 miles nearer to home, but would save me over an hour each way in travelling time. It was a busy station with the advantage of being easy to get to from Essex, where a lot of London firemen had moved to. Therefore, the waiting list to get there was very long, so no one thought I'd be going anywhere any time soon. So I put my transfer request in and pretty much forgot about it.

Some months before, I had applied for a junior officer's assessment centre. I'd already passed my leading fireman's theory and practical exams, so I had my 'ticket' for promotion; but then the LFB changed its promotion system. I'd been acting leading fireman on my watch, so wasn't worried about the assessment centre when my joining instructions came through. It would be a day of floor exercises, problem solving and interviews to see if you had the required leadership skills. I went along on the day, but wasn't too bothered either way and didn't treat it as seriously as some of the other candidates. The procedure was, you did your assessment and were marked for each part. Then, the results would be scrutinised and any potential junior officers would be contacted after a few weeks and offered a posting, where they would complete their development. At the end of the day, I was asked to go to the office to be interviewed again. I thought I was in trouble for not doing enough, because all the others were going home. I sat down in front of the assessors/trainers, who were all senior officers, not knowing what to expect. I was told that they had been impressed with my performance and would like to offer me a posting there and then. "No point in wasting time, we might as well get you going straight away", the most senior of them said. I hadn't expected this! I panicked and asked where I was going to be posted, my mind spinning, trying to think a way out of being posted off of the watch that I loved. "We haven't looked where the vacancies are yet, so we don't know". Thinking on my feet I said, "I'm really sorry, but I can't accept your offer. I've just put a transfer request in because I need to get nearer to home. I can't accept a posting that could be further away, or no closer. I might as well stay where I am." I then explained the circumstances which lead to my situation. They looked a bit puzzled; after all, it was unusual to offer someone a place on a development programme on the day of the assessment. It was even more unusual for the candidate to turn it down. They asked why I had bothered to turn up and, also, which station I had requested a transfer to. I told them that I'd turned up to see if I would be offered a posting in the future and, depending on where it was, I could then make my mind up whether to accept it or not. Then I told them which station I wanted. One of them said, "Yes, you and half the London Fire Brigade." I thought that was the end of it and left.

When I got home, my wife told me that an ADO someone or other had phoned a few times and wanted me to call him back ASAP.

When I did, he said "What if we promoted you onto a watch at your chosen station? Would you accept that?" I was taken back "Yes ,Sir, that would be great. Thank you." I came off the phone and told my wife, who was very happy, then my mind started racing. Tomorrow, I would have to tell my watch, the watch that I knew and loved, that I was leaving. I really was torn. My heart wanted to stay, but my mind told me that I needed to be closer to home. The next day, I went to work as normal but it felt like there was a cloud hanging over me. I didn't want to tell the watch that had taken me under its wing, taught me, helped me and supported me, that I was leaving. In the event, I didn't have to because our own ADO came into the mess while were all in it, drinking tea after our morning routines. He was a lovely bloke and everyone liked him. It wasn't unusual for him to come and have a cup of tea and chat with us. He came straight over to me and shook my hand. "Congratulations on your promotion, Steve, and well done for getting the posting you wanted." So the cat was out of the bag before I'd even had a chance to tell the watch. They were all pleased for me and understood my reasons for going, so a farewell night out was arranged for the following week between day shifts. I had been given the second day and both nights off on that tour as compensatory leave, because I'd be changing to the opposite watch. We worked the first day shift, then got ready and hit the town. It was a great night and we all crept back to stay at the station in the early hours. The next morning, I got up and made myself busy emptying my locker and gathering all my gear, while the others went about their morning routines. I had stand-easy, (Morning tea break), with them, then it was time to say goodbye. They came down to the appliance bay with me and there were handshakes and best wishes all round. I was choked and could hardly speak. The lump in my throat felt as big as a football. As I drove out of the yard, I saw them in my rear view mirror, waving at me and that was it; I couldn't hold the tears back any more and cried my eyes out. So many memories of being taught how to be a good fireman by them, of jobs we worked on together, the laughs and banter; I couldn't believe I was leaving it all behind. My time there was always very special to me, it still is and it always will be.

CHAPTER 6.

The wilderness years

Before I could start at my new station, I had to attend several courses which were supposed to help with my development. One was an outward bound course in Kent, which was a joke, to be honest. We were supposed to show and develop leadership skills by completing a range of pointless and silly tasks, taking it in turns being in charge. I found it hard to take seriously and couldn't wait for the week to end. Some of the things I saw made me question the brigades selection process, as at least half those on the course were absolutely useless. Simple decision making had their heads in a spin as they became bogged down with things that didn't matter and completely forgot about things that did. These individuals were given a cuddle and a pep talk from the trainers, instead of the bollocking they deserved. Eventually, the week came to an end and I went home. But I still couldn't join my new watch, because I then had to attend another weeks' course at the Fire Services College, in Moreton in the Marsh, Gloucestershire. I'd been there before when I finished my training at Southwark, before passing out and going to station. I loved it at the time, but it was my first taste of real firefighting in extreme heat and smoke; and it excited me. This time, however, was totally different. We were given incidents to be in charge of, which started off relatively minor but got more involved as the week went on. Moreton is a fantastic training facility. Built on an old airfield, it has fire stations, loads of appliances, real buildings including high rise, shopping malls, industrial units, basements, a concrete ship, real aircraft, trains and tankers, etc. There's even an oil rig there! The fires are built out of wooden pallets and straw bales, which created a lot of smoke and heat if they're kept bottled up.

At the incidents that were prepared for us there would be a candidate acting as OIC, (Officer in charge), and one acting as his deputy. The rest of the course would be the firefighters, who they would be in charge of and tell what to do. The thing is, we were always set up to fail. Bearing in mind that we had enough personnel to crew two fire engines, which were very poorly equipped, the incidents that the trainers set up for us were ridiculously complex. Fire in a high rise building with personas reported, fire in a shopping mall, fire in a workshop with acetylene cylinders involved, cars on a train track with a train crashed into them and multiple people trapped, fire in the sub-basement of a ship, multi vehicle pile ups with chemical tankers leaking. You name it, it was thrown at us. On most of the incidents, the candidate in charge would almost always immediately 'make it up', (request more fire engines), and ask for the attendance of specialist appliances; and every time were told that they were held up in traffic, or had crashed on the way. Any excuse was made to make sure you didn't get your make up appliances. So you'd have to deal with a major incident with two half stowed clapped out fire engines that belonged to the college. As if that wasn't enough, the trainers would throw more spanners in works to ruin your exercise. Like getting someone to hide in a nearby bush, saying they'd been thrown from a car, knowing that no one would dream of looking for casualties in a bush 100 yards away from the car accident; or waiting until you'd got miles of hose laid out at a fire, then, just as the crew was about to turn the hydrant on and charge it, telling you that the water main was burst and you've got no water. Bearing in mind that we were firefighters in London, all of these scenarios were total ridiculous. In real life, we would always get extra appliances when we requested them and we would never run out of water because of the amount of water mains and hydrants we had available to us.

To make matters worse, at the end of every exercise, the trainers would hold a thorough debrief, where they would stroll up and down in front of us, preening like peacocks, telling us how badly we'd performed. I grew to hate the trainers with a passion and started to speak up against them during debriefs. But the final straw for me came when they concocted the most laughable of all incidents for us to deal with. A helicopter crashed into an oil rig! Complete with chemicals, cylinders and running liquid on fire. The thing is, at the college, there was actually an oil rig with a helicopter embedded into it, but this set up was designed to train oil rig firefighters, not us! When we pulled up, I had to laugh at the scene that we were confronted with. They had made it look more realistic by igniting massive propane gas burners, so the whole thing was shrouded in flames – and there's us, with our two ancient fire engines. The candidate in charge lost all sense of reality and asked for another 8 pumps which he wasn't going to get, completely detached from the real world and not considering where in the North Sea these appliances would park; and that's assuming that our two were parked on a big boat that had taken us to the disaster! I was ordered to don BA, (breathing apparatus), and go to the rig to gather information about what was involved in the fire. I couldn't keep a straight face any longer and asked for a scuba diving set, instead. By now, the poor candidate in charge was totally gone and he didn't realise what I was getting at and what I was laughing at. Then, the penny dropped and he came back down to earth gradually. The whole exercise fell apart, which really annoyed the trainers. When they came over to our little gaggle, furious and demanding to know why we weren't doing something, I piped up and said that we're still waiting for the boat to take us to the rig, but it was unlikely to arrive, as it had been involved in an accident on the A406. The debrief for that one was very tense and, as was to become the norm in years to come, I couldn't keep my mouth shut. My rant started with, "First, we don't have any oil rigs in London. Two, if we did, the whole world would be mobilised if a helicopter crashed into it, not just us and out two crap fire engines and, third, don't be so fucking stupid. I can't remember how it finished, but it didn't go down too well and from then on, my card was marked. The good thing was that it encouraged more people on my course to speak up against stupidity. You see, back in the day, trainers were firefighters who had served a lot of years and were taking it easy for their last few before retiring. They'd get temporary promotion for becoming a trainer, so it boosted their pensions when the retired. Their experience and common sense approach was invaluable. But then the LFB decided that to be promoted to the higher ranks, people would have to spend a period of time in a specialist role, one of which was training. So, we got a lot of ambitious personalities, who were not particularly suited to station life, chasing promotion by going into training. There's an old saying which goes - Those that can, do. Those that can't, teach. - I think that's very true in the modern fire brigade.

At last, the week ended and I left Moreton with a different attitude to the one I went there with. But I wasn't out of the bullshit woods just yet; not by a long shot. There were more courses to attend before I could get back to being a (leading) fireman at my new station. One was held at Southwark training centre, where I had done my basic training and passed out from five years previously. It was all about management, or mismanagement, as I later called it. As junior officers, we would be in charge of crews and, sometimes, the whole station. They were trying to prepare us for that by teaching us all about management styles. In my experience, this isn't something that can be taught in a classroom. All the best and most respected Officers I had come across had learnt from experience, not by having an LFB microchip implanted in their brain. The trouble was, we had 'chipped up' trainers, trying to chip us up, too. These people had long since lost touch with reality, common sense and reason. Very few promotion candidates were strong enough and stubborn enough to avoid the dreaded chip from being implanted. The week entailed a series of lectures and role playing scenarios. One lecture was about the X and Y management styles. One, I can't remember whether it was X or Y, was getting the best out of people by treating them fairly and supporting them, the other was by ruling them with an iron fist. Anyone with any sense would understand that if you are good to people, generally, they'll be good to you, but if they think you're an arsehole, they'll treat you like one. I worked with both types of manager/officer over the years. Sadly, the arseholes among them always thought that the rank markings on their shoulders automatically gave them knowledge, experience, authority and respect. Nothing could be further from the truth. Trying to manage firemen is a bit like trying to herd cats. The good ones are strong characters with determination and inquiring minds that question everything and will quickly find any chink in someone's armour. A good officer, in my opinion, guides the watch and works with it to achieve the best outcome. I endured the week at Southwark and came away with an even worse opinion of the Brigade's new promotion process, but it still wasn't over.

The next course I had to attend was a watch trainer's course, which was held at Shoreditch training centre. As a junior officer, (JO), it would be my job to take care of training for my watch. In the real world, this used to happen by the Station Officer telling the JO to take the troops into the yard and do whatever training he thought they needed. Whether it was ladders, pumping, cutting or BA, it was something we did on a daily and nightly basis; and we enjoyed it because it pulled us all together and raised or spirits, as well as our ability as firemen. Every now and then, a new operational note would be released and we'd have a lecture on it, which usually turned into a watch discussion, where relevant past incidents were talked about. Now, as new JO's, we were being taught how to subject our watches to death by PowerPoint presentation, which was extremely dull and boring for everyone involved. Firemen have a very short attention span and if they aren't kept entertained they'll make their own entertainment, usually resulting contagious laughter, high jinks and a complete breakdown of the training package. The other thing we were told we had to do was create watch training packages. We'd have to put together 3 months' worth of training, which we were expected to stick to rigidly, and more or less mark each watch member on their performance. This didn't sit well with me at all. Firstly, our training was always dynamic and we practiced what we needed to practice. For example, if we had a difficult ladder pitch at a job and it didn't go smooth, we'd practice difficult pitches for a few weeks until we were all confident and working well together. Practicing pumps and pumping just because it was in the training programme was nonsense. As for marking each watch member on their performance and giving them extra training if they fell short on one or two occasions, that was totally counter-productive. If one or two watch members had a few weaknesses, we'd all work together on them without the rest of the watch even knowing about it. To me, that's the difference between a good watch officer and a chipped up robot. Having said that, I did come across one new addition to a watch that I served on who thought he was perfect, when he was far from it. He made mistake, after mistake, after mistake. Not minor ones, either. We all worked on the things he needed to brush up on, as a watch, but he would never acknowledge that he'd done anything wrong. The watch became frustrated with him, so the only option was to let him mess up on his own, with no one helping him. Maybe that way, it might have made him see that he wasn't so good after all. In the event, it didn't make any difference and he remained the useless, arrogant individual that he came to us as. In the end, he decided to climb the promotion ladder, the same as a lot of other useless firemen did over the years, to become an equally useless Officer. It might sound harsh, but there's a saying in the brigade; you can't polish a turd, you can only sprinkle glitter on it.

Finally, I'd completed all the courses required and went to my new station to join my new watch as their new leading fireman. But I still wasn't out of the wilderness yet.

CHAPTER 7.

All change part one.

The station that I'd been posted to was a good station. It was very busy with a good mixture of residential property, industrial estates, a couple of Hospitals, several underground and overground train stations, some very busy roads and even part of a motorway, which provided plenty of RTA's on a regular basis. I had heard that the watch I was going to be joining was a good, old experienced watch with some good hands and a few characters. It sounded not too different to the watch that I'd just left, so I was looking forward to joining them and getting on with the job following the previous few months of jumping through hoops. However, I was in for a bit of a shock when I arrived. The trouble with popular stations is that nobody leaves. Any vacancies that arise are usually dead man's shoes; which explains the long waiting lists to get to them. I had been lucky to secure the posting, partly through being bloody minded and not really caring whether I got the promotion or not, but partly because quite a few of the old watch had reached retirement age at around the same time and left the brigade for pastures new. This had left six or seven vacancies to be filled in a short period of time, which is very unusual. Usually, the turnover is much more gradual. They were filled with three new recruits, a fireman who had been on the waiting list for years, someone who was detached in on a temporary basis and me. We also had a young lad who would come to us from a very quiet station, to gain experience when they had enough spare riders to let him come. What was an old experienced watch, had become almost the opposite. There were a few good hands that were mid-career, as it were, but they were quiet, unassuming blokes and weren't used to being responsible for whipping the youngsters into shape. That was always the job of the older hands. The Station Officer was a lovely chap with many years' experience as a Station Officer, but he was weak. He was coming up to the end of his career and wanted a quiet life. The Sub Officer was hardly ever at the station because he was ordered to stand by in charge of other stations every shift, which is something that goes with the rank. So there I was, thrown into chaos from day one as a new leading fireman on a highly disrupted watch, at a very busy station.

Straight away, I missed the stability of my old watch, so I tried to carry on with what they had taught me and hoped that everyone would be happy with that. I was wrong, unfortunately. I was now on a young watch, half of whom had hardly any experience, with some very big egos. There was no pecking order and they had been left to their own devices. The old hands had retired; the other watch members were too nice to cause ripples and the Governor didn't want to do anything that might jeopardise his pension. Half the watch thought that they were the dog's bollocks and started to steer things the way they wanted them to go. It was a recipe for disaster. There was an upside to all this, too, though. Because it was now a largely young watch, we played a lot of volley ball, (traditional fire brigade game), which was always good fun and brought everyone together. Individually, all of them were nice people, but as a firefighting watch, the dynamics just didn't work, as I was soon to find out. My first few shouts with them were very minor shouts, so I saw nothing to raise any concerns. In fact, I embarrassed myself on the very first one. It was to an AFA, (automatic fire alarm actuating), and I was riding the back of the pump ladder. We pulled out of the station and no further than 200 yards down the road, I was fully rigged in my firegear, had my BA set on, straps tightened, released from the bracket and had my gloves and helmet in my hands, ready to go. I looked across to my fellow BA wearer to see him still pulling his boots on. He looked at me and laughed, "It's going to take us 5 minutes to get there mate". My first station's ground was little over a mile square and we had to be ready to go very quickly. This stations ground was vast compared to what I was used to and we usually had a lot more time to get ready en route. This was partly to explain why they had so many serious fires. House fires develop very quickly, so if it takes 5 minutes to get there, the fire is fully developed when you arrive. My new Guv, being of a slightly nervous disposition, had a reputation for making jobs up straight away, which also explained why this station had so many four, six and eight pump fires every year and was always near the top of the LFB league for make ups.

My first make up on the watch came after about a week. We had been called to a shed alight and, as the pump was off the run, I was riding the pump ladder along with a mish-mash of new personalities of mixed ability. When we arrived, the shed in question was 100% alight and the poor owner was trying to put it out with his garden hose. A hosereel was quickly pulled off the pump ladder and got to work. However, I noticed that the fire had spread into the conservatory of the bungalow next door which was full of paint pots, white spirit and other flammable materials, as it was undergoing a refurb. Within a very short space of time, the conservatory was fully alight and burning fiercely. I took the hosereel that was already in use and started to attack the fire, but it wasn't touching it, so I asked for a 45mm jet to be laid out. This is where things started to go very wrong.

I'll have to explain something here before I carry on. In the London Fire Brigade, we Dutch roll our hose. That means, when we make our hose up, we basically fold the length in half, so that both male and female couplings are together. The hose is then rolled up from the middle, so it ends up in a nice neat roll with both couplings on top. It is then stowed on the fire engine in such a way that when we need to use it again, we can just grab the roll, hold it by both couplings and bowl it out in front of us, then take the relevant coupling to where it needs to go. The cardinal rule here is, the female coupling always goes towards the fire;

because our branches and monitors have a male coupling. If you are running hose towards a hydrant, that's going away from the fire, so the male coupling goes there, as our hydrant stand pipes have female outlets. County Brigades never used to Dutch roll their hose because, back when they used canvas hose, folding it in half would cause the hose to degrade at the crease – especially if it wasn't unrolled for months on end. They just never moved on when we started using synthetic hose, for some reason. Instead, they'd roll the whole length of hose on one coupling, which made it take at least four times as long to lay out when it was needed. Crazy.

Anyway, I digress. I'd asked for a 45mm jet to be laid out and, in the meantime, carried on doing my best with the hosereel jet that I had. After a minute or so, which is a long time at a fire, there was still no sign of my jet apart from the branch that someone had dropped at my feet. After another minute and still nothing, I knew something had gone wrong, so I went to find out what was going on. As I came away from the conservatory, I could see that there was a lot of hose that had been laid out in all directions. I tried to find a female coupling, so that I could plug my branch into it and give the fire what for, but I couldn't find one. I traced the line of hose, which went all the way around the building, but couldn't find a break in it anywhere. This completely threw me - it still does to this day – and I struggled to get my head around it. Then I decided to try to find which part of the hose was coming from the delivery on the fire engine, so that I would know what hose I needed to plug my branch into. I went to the street and walked over to the rear pump bay of the fire engine, only to find two of my crew squaring up to each other! Things had obviously gone to rat shit and these two were more interested in blaming each other than sorting out the problem. I couldn't believe what I was seeing! After a bit of shouting and lots of fucks, I got them to focus on their job instead of their egos and set about sorting the problem with the water supply. In the meantime, the Guv had made pumps four. It turned out that two people, unbeknown to each other, had decided to lay out hose to supply my jet round the back of the bungalow. One went to the left hand side of the building and one to the right. Not ideal, but no biggy as these things happen, especially when the crew isn't used to working together as a team. The real problem arose because one of them had taken the male coupling around to the back of the building instead of the female. Someone else, seeing a male and female coupling laying in front of him, had connected them up. At the same time, someone had done exactly the same thing at the front of the building; so what we had was a nice loop of hose going all the way around the building with neither end connected to the fire engine - or the branch! In the time it took to realise what had gone wrong and get it sorted, the fire had reached the eves of the roof and was now in the loft space.

As we had enough charged hose to go twice around the building, thanks to the fiasco a few minutes earlier, two of us entered the bungalow with the jet to try to gain access to the loft, but we couldn't find a loft hatch in any of the rooms. Roof fires, when they go, go very quickly and you've got to be on your toes to stop them from getting away. I went outside and got a ladder to gain access to the roof itself. My idea was to make a hole in the roof to act as a fire break and to give us direct access to the fire. It's a good firefighting tactic when done properly and quickly. By now, some of the take machines, (make up appliances), had turned up and as I carried the ladder and started to pitch it to the roof, a station officer from another station, who I didn't know from Adam, asked what I was doing. When I told him, he said, "Well you don't want to make a hole right above the fire, do you. Take the ladder to the other end of the roof and make the hole there". In fact, above the fire was exactly where I wanted to make the hole. That way, the fire would vent straight up and out, without spreading, and we'd be able to hit it directly with our jet through the hole. Being questioned and given terrible orders by a station officer that I didn't know, plus the shenanigans since we'd arrived, I felt like I was fighting the fire on my own. And all the time it was getting bigger. I had a quick think and figured that I was the new boy on this watch and in this area, so I'd do as I was told. Two of us pitched the ladder at the far end of the roof and, straddling the ridge tiles, set about making a nice hole in it with fireman's axes. When the hole was big enough, I tried to direct water onto the fire, but the roof timbers in the way made it impossible; another good reason to make your hole as close to the fire as possible. Suddenly, I heard a loud whooshing, roaring noise and knew straight away what was happening. I instinctively got off the ridge and slid down the roof, stopping at the eves. I expected the bloke with me to be doing the same, but when I looked up, he was still sitting with a leg either side of the ridge, blissfully unaware of what was about to happen. I screamed at him, "GET DOWN HERE!! FUCKING GET DOWN NOW!!" Realising something must be wrong, he cocked one leg over the ridge and slid down the roof, right past me and ended up standing on the conservatory roof. At that moment, the fire burst through the hole that we'd made with almost explosive force and was now shooting skywards. It was totally predictable. We'd made an outlet for it and given it a lovely supply of oxygen. It was a very happy fire.

The natural reaction when you've had a close shave, is to laugh, strange as that may seem. I looked down at him and laughed, "That was close", then I looked down at his feet and under the pile of roof tiles that we'd just ripped off, I saw glass. The conservatory roof was made of glass. There wasn't time to shout anything this time, so I just reached out, grabbed him by his tunic and pulled him onto the eves of the proper roof with me. As I did, the glass broke and the conservatory roof collapsed and fell, along with all the tiles, into the fire below. This was game over for me. I'd done my best, but I was fighting a losing battle here. I was surrounded by idiots, it seemed. I got down off the roof, which was by now completely alight, and went out to the front of the building so I could take a break and take in what was actually happening. By now, a crowd had gathered outside and were venting their discontent. One of the neighbours was recording events with a video camera and one old woman, who made sure everyone knew that she was in the auxiliary fire brigade during the war, was shouting that we were shit and how the red hose was flat for ages before any water got through it. She was right, it was a shambles and I felt embarrassed. What was even more embarrassing was the sight of a Hydraulic platform trying to get sited in order to wash the bungalow down the road. My new Station Officer had ordered an aerial appliance in desperation, bless him, not taking into account the overhead telecommunications cables that made a pitch impossible. I was done. When we returned to the station, the people who were on the shout went off to do their own thing, mostly skulking off and taking themselves away from the rest of the watch. Everyone knew it had gone horribly wrong. I walked up to the mess to get a cup of tea, where I was met by the pump's crew who were fortunate enough to have missed this one. They laughed and asked me how it went. All I could do was shake my head in disbelief, which caused even more mirth among them. My reaction, apparently, is still remembered to this day.

CHAPTER 8.

All change part two

My first instinct was to get off of that watch and station as quickly as possible, but it was too late for that now. The vacancy I'd left on my old watch had been filled, anyway, and I had to keep reminding myself of the reason why I wanted to move stations in the first place. I was here now and had to just tough it out in the hope that things would improve. I tried to engage with the younger, inexperienced members of the watch and to pass on things that my first watch had passed on to me when I went there as a recruit. I thought they would be keen and interested, like I was as a buck. How wrong I was! One day, for example, I took the newest recruit down to the appliance bay to do some locker drills with him, the same as some of my old watch had done with me. I used to love doing them because not only was I being taught things that I hadn't been taught at training school, but they gave me the opportunity to ask loads of questions. Anyway, I was going through some knots and lines and testing him on what pieces of equipment were kept in each locker of the fire engines, but he just wasn't interested. I could see he was bored and didn't want to be down in the bay with me, learning his trade. I said to him, "Are you the slightest bit interested in what I'm showing you here, or would you rather be upstairs playing cards with the rest of them?" He looked at me and shrugged his shoulders, then said, "As far the Governor is concerned, we are all equal here. No one is any better than anyone else. We are all as good as each other." I was dumbfounded by his attitude, but wondered how much of it had been bred by a Station Officer who was too weak to get a grip of things on his own watch. I looked at him and said, "Well, I'm sorry to have to tell you this, but you're not as good as everyone else. In fact, you're not as good as anyone else. You've done six months and know fuck all." Then I closed all the lockers and went to speak to the governor. I relayed what had happened and asked him outright whether he'd been telling his recruits that they are as good as every other fireman on the watch? He sheepishly shrugged and said, "Well, what can you do? That's what these youngsters are like now days, they think they know it all and, to be fair to them, this is a busy station and they've had a few jobs since they've been here." I knew then that I was wasting my time. How can you hope to get the best out of someone, when they are being told by the bloke in charge that they are already the dog's bollocks? Who are they going to believe, me, or him?

I didn't give up, though and, eventually, things did start to change. But it was a slow and gradual process and I did alienate myself to some of the watch by being critical when I needed to be. The changes didn't happen overnight, though, they happened over years as various events unfolded. The first significant change was when the Station Officer went sick with stress and never returned. He was pensioned off on ill health in the end and we never saw him again. The Sub Officer acted up as temporary Station Officer for a while and he was bit more forthright, so it was nice to have a bit of back up when needed. But eventually, it all proved too much for him, too. Following a battle of wills with a very controversial character that joined our watch for a while, he went off sick with stress, too, never to be seen again. So we had a new set of officers and things did start to change gradually. Unable to get away with things that had previously been let slide, the wrong 'uns started to leave the watch one by one. At around the same time, I was offered temporary promotion at a neighbouring station, which was probably even busier than my own station, on a good old established watch. Their Station Officer was off on long term sick following an operation, so I was going there as a temp Sub O to be in charge of the station. It was a great watch, very experienced, good firemen and all nice blokes. They were also very funny and I loved my time there. But all good things come to an end and I returned to my own station and watch after about four or five months. But that spell of temporary had restored my faith in the LFB.

The next significant thing that happened was, our ADO, (Station Manager), either got promoted, or retired, I can't remember. I was a bit disappointed, because I liked him. He was as straight as a die. But his replacement was even better. He was a true fireman's fireman, even though he held a senior rank, and was well respected - for good reason. He was proper old school and the replacements for the blokes who had left were as good as handpicked. If anyone sensible recommended someone who wanted to get to this very sought after station, it was 'arranged', waiting list, or not. Within a matter of months, the dynamics of the watch totally changed. We had good experienced firemen joining us who were lovely people, too. They fitted straight in and were there because they wanted to be there. One thing that I was glad about, was that the youngsters stayed. Personally, I think they were always keen, but had been misguided by weak officers and shit firemen. Now, with decent Officers and good, experienced firemen to work alongside, they flourished. I saw them change from men who weren't that bothered about being good firemen, or simply didn't know how to be, to very switched on individuals who were mad keen and raring to go. In fact, one of them ended up reminding me of myself too much. I'd always been keen and loved being at the front, getting involved. Even as an Officer, I wanted to be all over the job and to see what was happening on all fronts. Given any opportunity, I'd grab a branch, or a Holmatro combi tool, and get stuck in at fires and RTA's. This particular bloke, no matter what we had, or where we were, would always be on my shoulder. If we were both on duty, I just knew that we'd end up working together at any jobs we might pick up. We would ignore orders from senior officers at big jobs and go about putting the fire out by doing our own thing. It was a lot of fun.

One particular 6 pump fire sticks in my mind. It was a derelict children's home that had been set alight; possibly by some of the former residents, who knows? It was a massive single story building consisting of many wings and corridors, with quadrangles throughout. We'd had a few smaller fires there previously but whoever had set the fire this time had done a proper job. There were several seats of fire and the building was burning well when we arrived. Because we had attended fires here before, we were familiar with the layout of the building. All the doors and windows had been boarded up and access was difficult, so me and my new right hand man run out loads of hose, pitched a short extension ladder to a flat roof, hauled all the hose up and asked for 'Water on'. The fire had burst through the pitched roof of an indoor swimming pool and we got the jet to work, attacking the fire from very close quarters. By now, the fire had also showed in several other parts of the massive building and the Governor had made pumps four. A senior Officer was ordered on and when he arrived, he made pumps six and started having kittens about us, up on the roof having a whale of a time. He started demanding that we come down as, according to a new and very stupid brigade policy, we shouldn't be working above ground level without a line rescue team! With that, he ordered a Fire Rescue Unit, (FRU), for line rescue! We were making good progress, as well as enjoying ourselves, so we decided that evasion was our best option and pulled up the short extension ladder onto the roof. Then, we lowered it into one of the quadrangles and went down, taking all the charged hose with us. Happy days! Now we were no longer above ground level, plus we could have even more fun, working our way along the corridors putting out room after room. We'd got a fair way in and were both getting a bit tired, to be fair, when we met the first BA crew coming in the opposite direction. By now, an entry point had been made and crews were being committed. The conversation still makes me laugh to this day. With voices muffled by their BA facemasks, they asked, "What the fuck are you two doing in here?" We replied, "We're waiting for you wankers to arrive. What kept you?" There was plenty of laughter between us all, then, we retraced our steps, back up on to the roof and made our way down and out. There was a bit of head shaking among the white helmets, but we didn't get the bollocking we were half expecting.

They say the Phoenix rises from the ashes and that's what happened with this watch. From the ruins, a great watch was formed. We were a very effective and respected firefighting watch in the area and, I'd like to think, we pulled quite a few jobs, on other station's grounds, around when they could have gone horribly wrong. I was glad I'd stayed and toughed it out. It might have taken years, but I was on a fantastic watch and I'd been there through the making of it. I did a few more stints as temporary Sub Officer at that station, but didn't particularly enjoy them because I was always ordered to stand by in charge at other stations. It does go with the rank, but I used to hate leaving my watch because I'd got to enjoy being on it so much. As most of the stations I was sent to were local, I used to bump into them at jobs from time to time and I was always glad to see them. But all good things come to an end. I got fed up with doing out duties and one night, after being ordered to station on the wrong side of London, I reverted and went back to being a leading fireman. A senior Officer turned up at the station, unannounced, within half an hour and called me into the office. He started trying to bollock me and demanded to know what was going on. I simply told him that temporary promotion is just that – temporary; and I'd decided that it ends tonight. There was nothing he could say to that, but as his parting shot he said, "You'll never act up again!" "Good!" I said, "I don't want to". It was a short lived victory for me, though, because after that, my life was made a misery for a fair while.

One day, a member of the watch that I really liked, unexpectedly transferred to the neighbouring station, which was pretty quiet compared to what we were used to. I was surprised, to say the least, and asked him why. He was fed up with a few things on the watch, but most of all he was fed up with the typical clientele that we served on our stations ground. We had a chat over a few beers and I could see his reasoning. I had stood by in charge of the station that he was going to, many times, and always enjoyed it. It was always a total contrast to my own station and it was nice being able to finish a meal, or a film, without being called out. It was even better getting a full nights' sleep with no disturbances, at least half the time. I always found my nights at that station to be very relaxing. It was the next best thing to getting a night off. Anyway, my mate said to me, "I've already spoken to our ADO about you coming here. He likes you and would like you to come. You'd love it". The nights at my station were killing me as I was getting older. It had started to take me two of my four days off to recover from two sleepless nights on our pump. Plus, I had become grumpy and snappy at home, which wasn't good. I thought about it for one more pint and said, "OK, I'll give it a try. But I'm not giving up my posting, just in case I don't like it", not really expecting anything to happen any time soon. The next tour, the ADO from the other station turned up at mine and, after having a word with my governor, called me into the office. "I've heard you want to come over to us for a while, to give it a try. If you're up for it, you can start next tour. I can give you at least three months and then see what happens". I was a bit taken back, but I thought fuck it, why not? I had nothing to lose. I'd only be detached there and could come back to my own station any time I wanted.

So, off I went to sleepy hollow and, straight away, felt the stress and tension leave my body and mind. It was everything I thought it would be, but I started feeling like a bit of a fraud; like a pretend fireman. While my mates at busy stations were out at all hours, dealing with all sorts, I was eating, watching a film or sleeping. It didn't feel right, even though we did get our own jobs from time to time and attended other stations' jobs. It was lovely, but just too relaxed compared to what I'd become used to. There is a bit of a stigma about being on a quiet station, but most of the blokes who served on them had transferred out after serving most of their time at the sharp end. It's almost a given, so no one ever questioned them or thought badly of them. But at this station, there were a lot of youngsters, across the watches who had been posted there from training school and didn't fancy life at the sharp end, so stayed there. That in itself is unusual, because recruits posted to quiet stations would normally put in for a transfer to a busier station at the earliest opportunity, in order to gain experience and do the job they joined to do. This spoke volumes about the quality of these people, to me. They were lazy and disinterested, as far as I was concerned, and just wanted a cushy life, while blokes twice their age were knackering themselves at the busy stations. It didn't sit well with me and I never really had a lot of time for them. But worse than them, were the youngsters who had transferred there from busier stations; something that used to be unheard of. Obviously, these individuals couldn't cope with life on a busy station and didn't have the benefit of time and experience on their side….and it showed! I missed the excitement of being at a busy ship and hated that this station was considered second rate. I told everyone that I was going to see the three months out and then I was going back to where I came from.

In the event, I didn't have to wait three months. On one of my rest days, the ADO called me and, very apologetically, informed me that the bloke I was covering had unexpectedly booked fit from a long term illness and I had to go back to my own station. I tried to sound disappointed, but inside I was as pleased as punch. I must have over done it with the disappointment act, because he told me not to worry, he'd do everything he could to get me back. So the next tour, I reported for duty at my own station and all the mayhem that went with it. For two or three tours, I was as happy as a pig in shit. Then I started to get tired and worn out again. The journey into work was a lot worse, too. The standard of driving in that part of London was diabolical, which made every journey to and from the station very stressful. The station and watch were great, but serving there wasn't doing my health any good at all. After a month, I phoned the ADO at sleepy hollow and asked him to do what he could to get me back there. He pulled all sorts of strings and, after a complicated three way move, I was posted there permanently. As I had to clear my locker and move all my stuff to my new posting, I took my young Daughter with me on one of my rest days, so she could help me and see my new station. She had been to my old station many times and even spent a Christmas afternoon there once. When we finished loaded my car, we set off for pastures new. She was keen to see Daddy's new fire station, but when we arrived her reaction wasn't what I was expecting. "Is that it? It looks like Trumpton. It's not a proper fire station, Dad, it hasn't even got an upstairs!" She never stopped taking the piss from that day onwards, using every opportunity to remind me that I was a fireman at sleepy hollow. Bless her.

But, as before, I had hopes that the watch could be turned around, even if the station couldn't. Between myself and my mate who had persuaded me to go there, we set about trying to recruit others from our old watch, or anyone else that we rated highly. We managed to get one, so we were now the three amigos and things started to look up. We then got another one join us, but he wasn't really our cup of tea at our previous station, so that was nothing to celebrate. A while down the line, we inherited two more who had served at a station that had just been closed by Boris Johnson, when he was London's Mayor. One was very good and one wasn't, but we were heading in the right direction. Some of the dross had left, so we did have the makings of a good watch, until we had a new Sub Officer dumped on us. He had been a new recruit at my last station and was the worst recruit I'd ever come across - and the worst fireman - but he'd jumped through all the hoops and got himself promoted and ended up as my Officer in charge. That killed it for me but, thankfully, I was close to retirement by then. I saw my days out at that station, which I regret. I always wanted to do the last six months at my previous station on my previous watch, but it wasn't to be. At my retirement do, the numbers were made up of blokes from my first two stations and watches, family and friends, which was perfect.

The burnt out flat at the ladder rescue job (B,S&T)

Assiting the London Ambulance Service.

Car under articulated tipper lorry. No serious casualties!

A different view of the London Underground.

STEPHEN CHARLES

At a 40 pump fire in Dagenham, 2012.

Miss Daisy and me after our BA wear at the 40pf. Note that the colour of the smoke is a lot lighter than it was before we were committed!

STEPHEN CHARLES

My last 6 pump fire, two months before I retired, where I was first in wearing BA.

My very last BA Job, one week before I retired.

Receiving my long service and good conduct medal from the Chief Officer at City Hall, London.

How my career started and finished. At STC in 1993 and packed away in two plastic bags in 2018.

CHAPTER 9.

STEPHEN CHARLES

Anxiety

As a temporary Sub Officer, I accepted the fact that I would be doing lots of out duties to be in charge at other stations. It goes with that rank. Most of the time, I enjoyed going out and working with firemen from neighbouring stations. There was no pressure on me to keep on top of their training programmes and other day to day station stuff, because that was the responsibility of their own Officer in charge. When you stand by in charge of a watch at another station, you are just a baby sitter, basically. My problems began when I started to be sent further and further afield, to stations grounds that I didn't know, working with firemen that I had never seen before, never mind worked alongside. Sometimes, I'd be driven by a stand by driver, who also didn't know the ground.

One such night, I was ordered to stand by at a station in a different area on the other side of London. I'd never even visited the place, so didn't know where it was. This was before the days of in car Sat Nav. It was a winter's night, pouring with rain and I had to negotiate heavy traffic, road works, diversions and one way systems, with only a paper back copy of the London A to Z, which I struggled to read in the glare of headlights and orange street lamps. When I arrived at the station, the watch had already eaten and all disappeared to do their own thing for the night. The only person still around was the Station Officer, which was odd because I thought I'd been sent in to be in charge for the night. It transpired that all they needed was a junior officer to ride in charge of their pump, but none of the watch had volunteered to act up for the night to keep it on the run, so I was sent in. Again, that's unusual. So, after testing my set and getting booked in, the pump went on the run and I went upstairs to chat with the Stn O. He seemed to be very laid back and was giving it big licks about what he had and hadn't done, what a good, old school governor he was and how much his watch loved him for it. I didn't know him from Adam, so had no reason to doubt him, but I thought to myself, 'They obviously don't love you that much mate, or you wouldn't be sitting in the TV room on your own talking to a stand by'. After I'd eaten, I found my room and got my bed down, even though I didn't expect to be in it for long that night, because this was a very busy station and I was riding in charge of the shit wagon.

Around 02.30 hrs, the bells went down. Hitting the bottom of the sliding pole, I could see the red and green bulbs illuminated in the appliance bay. Pump and Pump ladder mobilised. I went to the watchroom to see what we had and where it was and was I was handed a route card by the duty man, along with my copy of the tele-printer slip, which I read on the way to the pump. We had been called to a fire in a house, persons reported. As I mounted the machine, I was greeted by three people that I'd never seen before, because they weren't around when I arrived at the station, so there were very brief introductions all round as we pulled out of the station behind the pump ladder. Then the driver turned to me and said, "I hope you know the way, because I'm a stand by and don't have a clue where I'm going." In his infinite wisdom, the Stn O had decided to give himself the easy ride with a driver who knew the ground and put a stand by driver on the front of the pump with a stand by Officer. Thanks a lot! My driver did a pretty good job of keeping the pump ladder in sight and we managed to follow them, more or less, to the job. When we arrived it was pandemonium. Standard. It always is for the first minute or so at a proper job, until we get a grip of it and start bringing things under control. It was a big detached house and there was a lot of flame and smoke issuing from the upstairs windows. I can't remember every detail, because there's so much happening during the initial few minutes and you can't see what everyone is doing. You just have to trust the crew to be getting on with whatever needs doing until you've got a handle on the situation. I quickly established that there had been four people in the house. Three had got out before our arrival, but there was still someone in there. I went to report what I knew to the Stn O, but had no chance because he was up a short extension ladder trying to get in through the window with the most smoke and flame issuing from it! He had no BA on and no water. What he was trying to achieve, god only knows. But apart from what his thought process was, he was the Officer in charge and should have been direction operations, telling his crew what to do if they needed telling and getting things under control. Instead, he was on what seemed like a suicide mission and his blokes were shouting at him, "Come down Guv, for fuck sake. At least take a hosereel with you." I'd never seen anything like it. If someone had been hanging out of the window in need of being rescued, fair enough, but there wasn't. He was just being a dick. I decided very quickly that he was as good as useless and set about doing my job. Fuck him; if he got frazzled, serves him right. I did a very quick 360 of the building and found that the back of the house was pretty much untouched. I then entered the ground floor and went in as far as I could with no BA, making sure I could see clearly and breathe. There was a chance that the person inside had made it to the ground floor before collapsing. There was no fire on the ground floor, so I was able to do a quick search and was pretty certain that it was clear. So, in less than a minute, I'd established that the fire was on the first floor at the front of the building and relayed that information to the BA crew, who were just about to enter through the front door. My next thought was to locate the person still inside.

The three that had made it out were being treated on ambulances, so I opened the back door of one and climbed inside. There was a man in there with an oxygen mask on, but he was conscious and talking so I started gathering as much information as I could. "Who's still in there mate?" "It's my mum, she's 75 and disabled". "OK mate, where does she sleep?" "Upstairs in the back bedroom". "Left or right, looking at the back of the house?" "It's the one on the right". So I now knew where the fire was, where the old lady was and what was needed to get to her as quickly as possible. I had learnt from my brief 360 of the building that there was a window in what was probably the old lady's bedroom and that it was an easy ladder pitch to get to it. I tried to muster a few of the blokes outside and tell them to grab the ladder that the Stn O had been hanging off of a few minutes earlier and follow me, I know where she is. It was like I was invisible. I didn't even know their names and they didn't know me, so no one took much notice. As far as they were concerned, their legend of a Governor had told them to pitch the ladder to the front window – and that's where it was going to stay. I cursed under my breath and started to house the ladder on my own. I would go and find the old girl on my own if I had to. Thankfully, the persons reported message and the multiple calls that brigade control was receiving, resulted in another two machines being mobilised. They arrived just at the right time as far as I was concerned. The Officers and firemen who had just pulled up were keen to get involved. They saw the rank markings on my helmet and asked me what I needed. I told them and it was job done. Within a minute, the ladder was pitched to the rear window; two men had entered the bedroom and located the woman. Sadly, she was dead. They leant out of the window and told me the sad news. I went up and entered the bedroom, then called up the Stn O on my hand held radio to tell him. The bedroom was almost untouched by fire, so the woman had probably died from smoke inhalation. It was a sad sight and it did upset me for a minute or so. She was lying in bed, on her back with both hands gripping the covers, which she'd pulled up under her chin. The poor old girl, it appeared to me, knew something was badly wrong and was scared for the last few moments of her life.

The BA crew entered the room, after putting out the fire in the front bedrooms, so I climbed back out of the window and went down the ladder to speak in person to the Stn O and tell him what we'd found. By now, he was back on the pavement and trying to act like he had everything under control. The next thing I knew, he was gathering up his watch to take them upstairs to have a look at the 'stiff'. I followed them up, curious to see what this was all about. He got them stood all around the bed and proceeded to give them a run down on how she'd died, getting up close and personal, literally pointing things out to his captive audience. It made me angry to see him standing there, giving it Billy big bollocks now the incident was over, after embarrassing himself when we first arrived. I took myself away from it and went outside. I didn't want to boost his massive ego any more by giving him any of my attention. At fatal incidents, there is always a lot of standing about afterwards, waiting for a doctor to pronounce the casualty dead, the scene of crimes officers to rule out foul play, the fire investigation team to do their stuff and a brigade media resources officer to take photos and record the incident. During this time, the crews in attendance will make most of the gear up, and then stand chatting, etc. I didn't know anyone there. I didn't even know their names. They were stood about in groups of fives and sixes, as the job had been made up to four pumps and there was no work to do, but I stood on my own. I tried to latch on to a couple of groups, like the new boy on his first day at school, but they didn't know me and just carried on catching up with their mates from neighbouring stations without even acknowledging that I was there. Those moments are usually a good release for the stress and trauma of the job. Talking things through with others, comparing notes and hearing different perspectives, from different people, helps to tidy it all up and put things in some sort of order. I was left standing there in the rain with my own thoughts and wondering what the fuck I had just witnessed. It's not a great place to be and I hated the feeling of loneliness and isolation, even though I was surrounded by other firemen. Maybe there was an underlying issue that was making me feel this way, I don't know.

The next night, I was left on my own station to work with my own watch, but I couldn't really talk to them about last night, because they weren't there. I could tell them about it, but couldn't share it with them. That night, we picked up a fatal RTA on our own ground. A young lad had been T boned in his car and was dead when we got there. His sister was in the passenger seat next to him and she was very much alive and aware of what was happening. I helped to lift him out of the car, put him in a body bag and lift him onto the trolley that would take him away. It was another upsetting incident, the second in two consecutive nights; and even though I had learnt to distance myself from the personal and upsetting side of such incidents over the years, I felt my guard was gradually starting to slip. But then, these incidents happened during a very black period for me, during which I attended ten fatalities within a short space of time, which changed my whole outlook on life – and death.

Anxiety is a terrible, debilitating illness and those who have never suffered it, can never understand what it's like. Those who do suffer it don't know what's happening to them at first. To wake up at night, petrified and soaked in sweat, for no apparent reason; then, to sit in an armchair at home, frightened to move because the slightest movement amplifies the 'feeling' of being scared to death, but not knowing what of. It's extremely unsettling. When I was at my worst, I felt as if my skin was on fire, from head to foot and I couldn't think straight or reason properly. But the most bizarre thing about anxiety is; it can be triggered by very minor, everyday things that you wouldn't normally think twice about. You become hyper sensitive and aware, trying to cover every base to avert a tragedy that you are convinced is just around the corner and waiting to pounce on the unwary. You overthink everything just so you can stay ahead of the game and create problems in your mind that aren't even there, trying to pre-empt them and pre plan your actions. And it's a vicious circle. The more you over think, the worse your anxiety gets and the more non-existent problems you start trying to deal with in your mind. Trying to avoid every dangerous or distressing situation in everyday life is impossible, but you can't stop it, so you end up driving yourself, literally, mad. Your mind is jumbled and your body is almost paralysed. Make no mistake, anxiety is a very real mental illness and more people than you can imagine, suffer from it in various forms of severity. Some anxiety is normal and, more than that, a good thing. It's part of our built in survival instinct. Fight or flight, they both need adrenalin, which our bodies release as and when we need it. But when your body is being flooded with it 24 hours a day and you can't run and you can't fight to get rid of it, it's not such a good thing. It wears you out.

The strange thing is that it wasn't the incidents I attended that caused me to feel anxious. I was happy that I could deal with almost anything that was thrown at me on the fireground, although the fatal fire mentioned above did unsettle me a bit; because I felt like I was dealing with everything on my own and had become ultra-alert and aware. I had that job running around in my mind for ages afterwards, running over everything I could remember and wondering if I could have done more. Now, years later, I can obviously remember it in detail, so it still occupies a space somewhere in my head. Although the incident didn't traumatise me, it did cause me to become anxious every time I was sent somewhere unfamiliar to stand by after that, because I feared a repeat of the same sort of situation. Looking back, maybe that was a trigger for the start of my problems – I don't know.

But my extreme anxiety was caused by a number of things that were out of my control; and not being in control was what frightened me the most. When my Daughter was born, I was petrified that something bad was going to happen to her when I wasn't there, or of not being able to help her if she needed me. Losing my first child had affected me deeply and, I suppose, this was a knock on effect. I had been utterly useless back then, unable to help my Son when he needed me the most. I never got over that – and never wanted to be that useless again. Therefore, when my shifts finished, all I wanted to do was get in my car and get home to see my Daughter. Although I had transferred to a station closer to home, it was still an hour and a half drive. If there was a hold up on the A12, it could take three or more hours to get through it, during which I'd start to panic because I couldn't get home. Most of my out duties were to nearby stations or stations that were even closer to home but, every now and then, I'd be sent to the arsehole of the universe on the other side of London. Sometimes, it could take two hours just to get back to my own station at the end of the shift, because of gridlocked traffic in certain parts of the Capital and then there was still my usual hour and a half drive home from there. I hated these out duties because, to me, they were keeping me from my Daughter and, therefore, in my mind, putting her in danger. Irrational, I know, but that's what anxiety does to you. I remember leaving one such station at the end of my shift and immediately getting stuck in a huge traffic jam, caused by emergency road works. I was a very long way from home, but I seriously considered abandoning my car and walking home, because at least I'd be getting nearer with every step instead of sitting motionless in a state of extreme anxiety. The butterflies in my stomach felt like a flock of seagulls, my skin felt like it was alight and my eyes felt like they were going to pop out of my head. When I realised that my car was still going to get me home quicker than my feet, I felt like crying. I was stuck there and there was nothing I could do; and all the while, I was imagining all sorts of things going wrong at home, which just fed the beast even more.

Thankfully, these horrible occurrences didn't happen very often, right up until the point when I busted myself from temporary Sub O and reverted to leading fireman. I did it because I figured life would be a lot less stressful if I was getting less out duties. By now, most station administration was computerised and we would have to check the computer at the start of each shift to see what out duties there were and who was going where. To me, it was like playing Russian roulette. Sometimes, I'd be almost too frightened to click on the button to reveal where I had been ordered to stand by. As a Sub O, you are sent out almost every shift, but as a leading fireman, out duties are rare. On the night that I busted myself, a particularly nasty leading fireman out duty was sent across from the staff office within minutes. I knew that management had the hump, but I didn't expect such a quick reaction. I went mad and, in the end, my governor phoned them up and got it cancelled. But that was just the beginning. After that, I was being hit with horrible leading fireman out duties almost every shift. So apart from the anxiety that they caused, I was getting even more from knowing that someone up above had decided that I needed to be given a hard time for daring to revert back to my substantive rank. At the time, I was getting it from all angles and just driving to work became an epic ordeal because as I got closer to the station, my anxiety would build to unimaginable levels, wondering what they had in store for me today. Something had to give. I knew that it was pointless complaining, so I set about proving that I was being singled out for special treatment, which turned out to be surprisingly easy.

I hated all the station admin being computerised, but it did have its advantages sometimes. If you were determined enough and willing to do a bit of digging on the system, you could access a list of all the stations that were short of staff on any particular shift and see where their standby was being sent in from. I knew something wasn't right, but I was shocked when I saw what was actually happening. I was regularly being sent out of my own area, even though there were local stations that needed someone in for the shift and, more importantly, there were spare personnel in the areas that I was being sent to who could have been sent in to cover. I printed off these reports over a period of time and, when I thought the time was right, I went to the Divisional Officer's office with them. He was someone that I already had no respect for, because he was a useless individual and, from people who knew him as a fireman, always had been. But he'd got himself promoted out of trouble and thought his rank markings, which he often pointed to when asserting his authority, gave him magic powers. I knocked on his door and entered his office. He leant back in his chair, folding his arms across his fat belly, "And to what do I owe this pleasure, Steve?" He got my back up straight away. "Well, I'm being singled out for special treatment by someone in the staff office and being clobbered for more out duties than any other leading fireman north of the Thames, plus they're all over the place and I'm not fucking having it anymore". He gave me a smug look and started trying to give me a lecture on the brigade's obligation to provide fire cover to the whole of London and how we have to go where ever we are needed to cover staff shortages. As usual, he was reading from a memorised book. I let him finish his first sentence and stopped him. "Right, stop there before you embarrass yourself. You know what's going on and I want you to stop it". He shrugged and said, "I don't know what you're talking about". I threw the pages that I'd printed off for the last few weeks on his desk in front of him. He picked them up and skim read them, I'd highlighted the relevant parts. "OK, that does look a bit unusual, I have to admit". His demeanour changed from being a cocky senior officer to that of a schoolboy who's been caught stealing sweets. "Right, it's unusual, you say. I can think of other terms to describe what's been happening and I want it to stop", I said. He tidied the pages I'd tossed him and said, "Leave it with me". Things did return to some sort of normality after that but, by then, the damage was already done. Clicking on the out duty button on the computer still filled me with dread, followed by either relief, or a heightened state of anxiety, depending on whether I was spending the shift on my own station, or being sent out. The level of anxiety was directly connected to where I was being sent to and how long I envisaged it taking me to get home from there at the end of the shift.

It sounds ridiculous now, as do most things that cause people to suffer from anxiety when thought about in a rational manner, but no amount of rational thinking stopped the process. I was spinning out of control in a vicious circle of overthinking, producing too much adrenaline, which induced more overthinking and worrying, which produced more adrenalin and so on. The physical effects of which, were horrendous. I had to try to find a way of breaking the cycle, so when my mate contacted me and asked if I'd like to join him at the station that he'd just transferred to, I gave it more consideration than I normally would have done. It was a quieter station but, more importantly, it only had one appliance. At one appliance stations, the leading fireman always rides the back of the pump ladder, always rigs in BA for jobs and, more importantly for me, doesn't do any out duties. Of course, after weighing up the pros and cons, I decided to give it a go. It seemed like the perfect solution to my problem, plus, this station was nearer to home, too. For the first few months, it was great and panned out just like I'd hoped it would. I started to relax and get some sort of normality back into my life. Then things changed. The brigade wanted to change our shifts to some horrendous new pattern that would have turned my home life upside down, along with that of every other firefighter in London. Our Union fought the proposal, obviously, but that lead to a very long and bitter dispute, which dragged me to even lower depths of despair and anxiety. The brigade decided to aim it's venom at leading firemen in the hope that, by breaking us, they would break the resolve of all operational firefighters, get their own way and put an early end to the dispute. It was the classic divide and conquer tactic, but they hadn't taken into account the loyalty that we all had towards each other. We, (leading firemen), were given orders that we had no choice but to disobey because, if we had carried them out, we would then leave our colleagues open to charges and disciplinary action. The brigade retaliated by stopping percentages of our pay for what they said was partial performance. At first, we were stopped 20% of our pay, which really stung right on top of Christmas. But our mates started having collections to support us and make up the shortfall in our wages. Realising that their initial plan hadn't worked, they, (by 'they', I'm referring a small, very vindictive and nasty group of principal officers and HR civvies), started to issue us with more illegal orders to carry out. A refusal resulted in a further 20% reduction in wages for every order that was disobeyed. Some leading firemen were being docked 60% of their wages before the dispute ended; and end it did, as they all do eventually, with a compromise. It took years, but our Union took the brigade to court over the illegal stoppages of pay and it had to pay back the money it robbed, but most of the individuals who were responsible for causing such bitterness had either retired from or left the LFB, as had a lot of the junior officers who had been subjected to their venom. It was during this dispute that I was first signed off by my GP with work related stress, anxiety and depression.

My Doctor had signed me off for a month, straight away, which was quickly picked up on by the brigade. As soon as mental health issues are highlighted, the occupational health team are notified and you are then referred to a specialist. I can honestly say, hand on heart, that the OH team was excellent. I was supported totally and felt as if I had a big, warm comfort blanket wrapped around me. These people were medical professionals, whose main concern was our health and wellbeing. Jumped up and vindictive brigade officers couldn't argue with them, no matter how much it frustrated them and, more importantly, they couldn't get to you unless you wanted them to. My GP had initially referred me to a local counselling service, because she thought it would benefit me. I went along because I thought it might benefit me, too. After two sessions, I couldn't see the point of it. The councillor didn't have a clue what I was talking about and offered no solutions. All he did was to listen and give me sympathy. When you're suffering from complex mental health issues, sympathy doesn't make them better. What you need is a way out of your suffering, positive action and results. I referred myself to the brigade's own counselling service, in the hope that they might be able to offer something more useful. I'd had a few sessions with them following the loss of my Son and held them in high regard. From the moment I sat down and started talking at my first session, I knew that they would be able to help me. The counsellor assigned to me was on a different level to anyone I'd spoken to before. She understood exactly what I was saying and assured me that I wasn't the only junior officer having the same issues. She gained my trust instantly and future appointments were arranged. After three months, I wanted to go back to work; not because I felt whole lot better, but because the brigade's policy was that after three months off sick, your base posting would be made vacant and filled by someone on the waiting list for your station. You would then be posted where ever there was a vacancy on your return to work, no matter where it was in London. To me, it didn't make sense to create a vacancy and then fill another one somewhere else with the person who had been ousted from their own watch and station. But then, in my opinion, this policy wasn't about making sense, it was used as a punishment to discourage sickness. Either way, I was fast approaching the deadline and the last thing I wanted was to be posted somewhere further away from home. Just the thought of it exacerbated my anxiety, but each time I asked the consultant to book me fit, he refused and signed me off again, saying I wasn't ready to go back to work yet. I explained my problem to him and he told me not to worry and assured me that I wouldn't lose my posting. Such was the power of the occupational health service. Eventually, he reluctantly allowed me to go back, but I was still under his care and had to go back for periodical assessments.

Every week, in between my night shifts, I'd get the train to Southwark for another hours counselling session. Usually, under normal circumstances, we would only be allowed to have six sessions, but my counselling went on for two years. After each block of six, my counsellor would apply to the brigade for another block because she recognised that my issues were somewhat complex. The reason why I went in the first instance paled into insignificance as she dug away the layers of my mind, uncovering things that I thought I'd long forgotten about or that I had dealt with and pushed out of my memory. It got to the point where we'd be going round in circles. Every time her questioning got too tough, I'd clam up and say nothing. One day, she asked me whether I'd ever heard of EMDR therapy and whether I'd be willing to give it a try. I hadn't and agreed to have a go. EMDR is Eye Movement Desensitisation Reprogramming. It's too complex to detail in this book but, basically, it releases terrible things that people have locked away somewhere in their brain, because the event, or events, were too traumatic to think about and deal with at the time. In time, we don't even realise that we have these terrible memories in our heads, because every time they rear their ugly head, we push them back again. I was warned that it wouldn't be easy and, before the therapy even started, the first thing I was told to do was, remember a time when I felt totally happy, secure and relaxed and remember every detail of it. Where it was, what it smelt like, how it looked, how it felt, etc. Once my counsellor/therapist was confident that I had this place firmly implanted in the front of my mind, she told me that this was my safe place and that after every EMDR session, she would take me back there before letting me go. I couldn't see the significance of it at the time, but she seemed very serious about; and I trusted her. The therapy went on for a few months and, looking back on it, she would take me to the brink, then back to my safe place. Each time, the brink got further away from what I was comfortable with. One day, she said. "We've got another three sessions to go and then we're going to have to end this. How do you feel about that?" I didn't really know how I felt, to be honest. My next session was a little more brutal and probing than usual. I felt a bit rattled by the depth of questioning, but was brought back to my safe place before the end, as usual. I wasn't prepared for what happened the following week. Instead of stopping the questions before things got too distressing, she kept asking for more details. I told her what I could remember, but that wasn't enough, she kept asking me to describe, in detail, everything I was telling her. How did that feel? What did you hear? What did you think? What did you do? What did you say? Who was with you? What did they say? Suddenly and without warning, I was sitting in the delivery room in Colchester Maternity hospital. I heard the footsteps coming along the corridor, I saw the door open and the group of doctors and nurses come in, I could see their faces and hear their voices. I remembered every word they said and every word that I said I remembered the phone calls that I made to family and I remember the consultant coming to see me once he'd finished stitching my wife up after saving her life, still dressed in his scrubs. I remembered seeing my boy for the first and last time. But these weren't just memories; it was like I was back there experiencing it all over again. I broke down and cried out in pain, like I'd wanted to at the time but couldn't. I threw my head into my hands and pulled at my hair, sobbing uncontrollably. At the time, I couldn't even manage to shed a tear, because it was so surreal and I didn't want to believe, couldn't believe, it had happened. She left me to cry for a while with no interruptions, then, she slowly brought me back to my safe place. I felt exhausted but, somehow, calm. When I sorted myself out and looked up at her, I saw that she had been crying, too. My last appointment was a very brief one. It was just a chat and I was asked how I'd been and how I felt. No mention of anything traumatic and no probing questions. When I got up to leave for the last time, we hugged each other. Probably a big taboo, professionally, but I'd laid open my soul to this woman over the last two years and, probably, burdened her with my problems. She thanked me for trusting her and that was the last we saw of each other.

Before that day, I was unable to speak openly about the event without choking up, my throat tightening and tears welling up in my eyes, before having to walk away from whoever I was talking to at the time because I didn't want them to know just how deeply I'd been affected. Now, I could talk to people about it and explain in more detail what actually happened. However, that didn't put an end to all my anxiety issues. While I was going for counselling and under the care of the occupational health service, I had been excused from doing out duties because it was known that they were causing me problems and not helping with my recovery. This didn't sit well with certain elements of senior management, bearing in mind that as a leading fireman serving at a one appliance station, I shouldn't have been doing them, anyway. The reason that I had been was mismanagement on the brigade's part, but that didn't stop the knives from coming out when the counselling sessions and appointments with OHU came to an end. I was soon being sent all over the place again and, even though the trauma of losing my son had now been dealt with, the anxiety about the possibility of losing my daughter, real or imagined, was still extreme. I started to slip backwards again but was determined to fight it and beat it, so I battled on. No matter what station I was sent to, the first question I always asked when I got there was, "What time does the leading fireman on the next watch usually get in?" Sometimes, the leading hand would get in early and jump for the standby, (get the standby away and ride his position on the machine before going on duty). Most of the time, someone got me away and this was always a huge relief. However, there were a few stations where this didn't happen and the leading hand would turn up either bang on time, or late. On these occasions, I'd get myself wound up and end up pacing the station until I could leave. Sometimes, I'd even get my fire gear off the machine and load my car up to get a flying start once the change of watch bells went down. Even though I was trying to fight it and think logically, it was eating me up more and more, week by week. My drive to work was stressful enough as it was, because the main route I had to take into London was the A12, which was notorious for accidents, traffic jams and road closures; any one of which would make me late for work and bring more stress due to the brigades new breed of management and it's crazy absence control policy. If you were late three times in a year, you'd be disciplined, regardless of what the circumstances were.

One morning, I was driving to work when my car started to lose power and died. I was so paranoid about breaking down because one, I was a good time keeper and hated being late for anything and, two, because breaking down on the journey home would prevent me from being where I was needed. Therefore, I used to carry spare fuel filters, drive belts and a full set of tools in the back of my car, just in case. I always used to allow plenty of time for my journey to work, for the reasons above. I was soon checking the car for anything obvious; it felt like a fuel problem the way it gradually died, so I changed the diesel filter and primed the system. Still, it wouldn't start, so I was under the car lying on a wet road in the pissing rain, tracing the fuel lines back to the tank.

I couldn't find anything, so phoned the RAC out to get me going again. Then I phoned the fire station to let them know that I was going to be delayed due to transport difficulties. No problem there as I hadn't been late this year yet. The RAC turned up pretty quickly but, after trying for half an hour, couldn't get me going and called for a recovery truck. I knew that I wouldn't make it to work that morning, so I phoned the station and asked for the station manager. He was a mate of mine and we'd known each other since we were both firemen, so I was expecting a bit of understanding from him. "Hello mate, I've broken down on the A12. The RAC couldn't get me going again and are going to recover my car. Can I request an emergency PH, (Day's leave), as I won't be able to get in today?" I was expecting a positive response and for him to tell me that he'd take care of it. That's how things used to work. How wrong I was. "No Steve, they won't grant you a PH because they're short of officers, so you'll have to come in." I couldn't believe it. "So, how shall I get there? Walk? I'm about 20 miles away! Then, even if I walked, what happens to my car? They won't recover it if I'm not here and, then, I've still got to get to whatever shit out duty they're going to send me on today and back, then find a way of getting back to my car before being recovered. It's impossible mate." By now, I was in despair; that's anxiety for you. Any rational thinking person would have booked sick and to hell with it. But when you're suffering from mental health issues like this, you worry about everything, to the extent that you start to imagine every possible negative outcome. I asked him, "What's my sickness record like?" thinking I might have to use sickness to cover my absence. "No mate, you've had too much sick already this year, what with you being off with stress and all that, so you'll be on a warning if you go down that road. You'll just have to book delayed and, when you finally get home, make your way to work on public transport". Basically, I was in a no win situation. Under normal circumstances, I'd have shrugged my shoulders and forgot about work for that day, but my mind was in turmoil and instead of getting a bit of help and support from my 'mate', the station manager, I was getting obstruction and officiousness. After sitting in my car for two hours, waiting for the recovery truck, I was eventually on my way home. As soon as I got there, I set about fixing my car so that I had a way of getting to work the next day. It turned out to be something simple, that both I and the RAC man had missed, but by the time I'd figured it out, it was way too late to drive to work for the remainder of my shift.

That little episode, on top of everything else that had been going on, really rattled me, even though it was really nothing to get worked up about in the grand scheme of things. The next day, I drove to work on tenterhooks, frightened of breaking down again. On arrival, I got showered as usual and went to the mess to make myself a coffee. On the way over, I bumped into my temporary Station Officer. Again, I'd known him for years and he was a mate. At one time, I'd been his OIC when I was a temporary Sub O and he was a fireman. He was a bit mad, but a lovely fella if he liked you. He looked at me and said, "You OK, Steve? You don't look right mate". I stopped and said, "I've been better mate. I'm struggling to keep it all together, to be honest" and told him about yesterday's episode. He recognised the signs, because he'd suffered himself in the past. "I'll take you off the run mate and you can hang about here, or go home, do what you like, but you need to get your head together". I said, "No, I'm alright, honestly. I'm just letting you know that I'm struggling a bit and need to shut myself away for a while. If we pick anything up, I'll be fine, you know that". I went back to my room, closed the door and lay down on my bed, trying to keep still and keep the anxiety under control. I missed roll call and he tested my BA set for me. Then, there was a knock on the door and he told me to come with him to the station manager's office. Even though I hadn't wanted him to, he had, quite rightly, told my station manager and I had to go before him. My mate came in with me and I was glad of his support I sat down and then just choked up. My throat was tight and I couldn't speak. My eyes were bulging as I stared at the wall, trying to stop tears. The station manager said, "Mate, you need to come off the run and take some more time out." Now, after being a total tosser the day before, he was calling me mate! This made me angry and my mood suddenly changed. "No, fuck you! I'm not taking any more time out. Yesterday, you didn't give a fuck and just made a difficult situation even more difficult for me, when you could have helped. Now you're concerned? You can go fuck yourself". My temp Stn O stepped in and said, "Steve, I've been where you are, many times before. In fact, I've been further than you have. I've actually stood on a station platform waiting for the next train to come in to jump under it. I'm pleading with you mate, take time out and get back on the tablets. You owe it to your family, believe me". I'd never contemplated suicide, not once; I wanted to be around for my daughter and the rest of my family, so that was never an option for me. But his words resonated with me. He was a good fireman and a good friend. I liked and respected him, yet here he was, laying open his soul to try to help me. In the end, we came to a compromise. Leave me alone today and see how I feel tomorrow, but don't take me off the run. I spent the rest of the day lying on my bed. We tipped out once, I think, to an AFA. I was fine, but too embarrassed to look at or speak to any of my watch. They all realised something was badly wrong, but didn't mention anything to me. I slept at the station that night and when I woke up the next morning, the anxiety had climbed to another level. I walked into the station manager's office and said, "I can't do it today, I'm going home". I think he was more relieved than I was. So, off I went, back to the doctors and got signed off again.

I was referred back to Occupational Health and when I walked into the consultant's room, he was surprised to see me. He seemed genuinely upset and concerned that I'd ended up back there. After I'd been through everything with him, he typed out my report as he usually did. In it, he would give his assessment of my mental health and suggest any measures that could implemented to make things better for me. He would give me a hard copy and email a copy to the brigade. In this report, he suggested that I be excused from doing out duties, as they were a major contributing factor to my anxiety. It was agreed by management, but they wanted to review the decision on a regular basis. When I went back to work, I was placed on light duties for two weeks. As soon as the two weeks was up, the staff office sent over an out duty for me. My Stn O phoned them up and explained the situation to them, which they couldn't understand and questioned him, asking who made the decision and under whose authority. They weren't happy bunnies when they found out that it had come from an authority that was much higher than them, but just had to swallow it. Every couple of months or so, I was visited on station by the Head of HR, (Human Resources), for a periodical review of the situation. She was brilliant and didn't have any agenda other than my wellbeing. After each review, my being excused from out duties was extended. She kept the Wolves from the door, so to speak. This went on for a few years and then, one day, I was sent to see a psychologist by the brigade. I went for my appointment and he listened to what I had to say before giving me a lengthy explanation of various stress triggers and how they can cause extreme anxiety and depression. It all made sense to me and I was quite relieved to discover that I wasn't a unique case. The Psychologist typed my report and recommended that my trigger, out duties, be ceased indefinitely. I was happy, but the same couldn't be said for certain senior officers, who thought I was trying to get one over on them. My old Station manager, who had by now been promoted 'up the road' and worked out of HQ, came to my station for a random visit, or so he said. He waited until I was alone with him and said, "When are you going to start doing out duties again? Come on, you've had a good run, it's been a couple of years now." I looked him straight in the eyes and said, "A good run? That's not how I see it" and walked away from him in disgust. A few weeks later, I was sent to see an independent Psychiatrist in West London. This man had nothing to do with the brigade, specifically, but was used by Civil Services like the Police, Military, Ambulance and any other services where people suffered work related mental illness. This was a very lengthy consultation, but was more like a friendly chat than an interrogation. At the end of it, I couldn't help it and had to ask, "So, am I mad then?" He laughed and said, "No, not at all. You're a well-balanced individual. It's like this; if you can't eat Brussels sprouts because they make you sick, don't eat them. It's as simple as that." Then he got on with typing his report, which I read on the train on the way back to my station. I was amazed at how clear cut he made the situation. He said I was a mentally balanced, intelligent man with well-developed social skills and a personable nature. He also recommended that I be left alone to get on with my career without the threat of the thing that triggered my anxiety. By the time I got back, his emailed report had been delivered to my Stn O and every other Officer above who was relevant. I still believe that certain elements within the brigade were trying to find a chink in my armour and expose me as someone who was swinging the lead. Inadvertently, they had done me a huge favour by reinforcing my position and putting me beyond the reach of their vindictiveness. I still got my visits from the Head of HR, but all we did was talk about our mutual love of horses for an hour whenever she turned up. She was great and very supportive. Eventually, because the brigade was putting pressure on her to get me to do out duties again, I agreed to her strategy to get them off her back. She suggested that I do only two out duties a month and only to stations that were closer to home. By now, my daughter had left school and become independent and I actually enjoyed the few out duties I did in my last couple of years' service. They were local, so I knew everyone and I wouldn't have to worry about getting home. If certain Officers had been interested in working out a solution, instead of keep beating me with a big stick and making things worse, it would have saved us all 8 years of grief.

CHAPTER 10.

Fire safety

I was walking across the appliance bay one morning after completing my daily routines, when I was stopped by our ADO, (station manager). He was a lovely man and old school fireman's fireman, liked and well respected by everyone from the firemen on station, to the higher echelons of LFB management; a true gentleman. "Morning, Steve. You alright?" I smiled and said, "Yes thanks, Guv, you?" He smiled back and said, "Yes, good thanks. If you've got a minute, can you pop into my office for a chat? Get yourself a cup of tea first. I have two sugars in mine." I was a bit puzzled, but went up to the mess and made us both a cup of tea, then took them to his office. I sat down opposite him. "No biscuits?" he laughed, then went on, "I've noticed that you don't seem yourself lately, is everything alright? I felt a twinge of emotion but said, "Yes Guv, everything's fine" but my armour had been chipped by someone showing some concern for my wellbeing and I unexpectedly started to well up. He looked at me and said, "I think you need to take a bit of time out mate. If you don't, you're going to have a breakdown. I've seen it before and I've been keeping an eye on you." A tear got away and rolled down my cheek, quickly brushed away in the hope he didn't notice. "Nah, I'm fine Guv, honestly. I've got a bit of shit going on right now, but I'm alright." Then we had a little chat about the issues I had and the need I felt to get home as soon as possible after each shift, for my daughter. He seemed to understand and then said, "Have you thought about going into Fire Safety? I did it for years and it's the best job in the brigade. It's a nine day fortnight and you'll be home sunbathing in your garden by 12.00 every day. No nights and no weekends or bank holidays, it'll suit you down to the ground." My ears suddenly pricked up. I'd never even considered a career in the brigade that didn't involve being on a station, but this sounded fantastic. It was about to get better. "I've got contacts there and could get you detached in for at least three months. If you like it and decide to stay, that could be arranged, too. If you did stay, you'd be bumped up two ranks to Station Officer, so you'd be earning bigger wages and retire on a bigger pension, plus there's plenty of opportunity for further promotion." That was it. He'd sold it to me, totally.

I thanked him and shook his hand as I left his office, then I went to tell the exciting news to my watch in the mess. "I might be going into Fire safety for a while", I said. The mess erupted in laughter; I think someone even spat their tea across the table. "Fuck off, Steve! You, in Fire safety?" followed by even more laughter, "Sit down mate, you're obviously not well, someone, put another sugar in his tea, for fuck sake". I held my hands up and admitted that it wasn't really me, but then told them of all the benefits. "Listen, it's a nine day fortnight, no more nights, weekends or bank holidays, plus, you get home by 12.00 every day. I'll get bumped up to Stn O, so it's more money, too. What's not to like?" Just then, the ADO came into the mess and said, "OK, Steve, it's all sorted. Report to East Ham Fire safety at 09.00 tomorrow morning. You won't need to take your firegear or bedding with you." Suddenly, the laughter died down and once the ADO left the mess, my watch started asking questions. "How did you wangle that, you jammy bastard? When you get your feet under the table, try to get me in there will you?" I felt as though I'd had the last laugh - or had I?

East Ham fire safety offices were attached to the fire station in High Street South. The journey there was longer than it was to my home station, but getting up and leaving earlier in the mornings wasn't such a big deal if I was going to home by lunchtime every day. I was up bright and early the next day, full of enthusiasm;

still pinching myself because it all sounded too good to be true. Even the rush hour traffic on the A13 didn't dampen my spirits too much. I walked into the ADO fire safety's office and introduced myself. He seemed a very nice bloke and had obviously done me a favour by detaching me into his department. He shook my hand and said, "We'll have a proper chat later on, but have you got any questions?" I was stood in front of him in my civvies, with sleep in my eyes and stubble on my chin. I always used to get showered, shaved and changed at work, so I asked him where the showers and locker room were. He looked slightly bemused and replied, "Oh, there are no facilities like that here. I think there's a shower in the Woman's toilet; I suppose you could use that, as long as you let everyone know you're in there." So, off I trotted to the ladies toilet to get ready. It was tiny! One cubicle, a sink and small shower, with no benches or clothes hooks. It was a bit of an ordeal, but I got myself sorted out for work and made a mental note to get ready at home in future. As I came out, I was met by the ADO who said, "Come on, I'll show you the kitchen and then take you to meet the blokes you'll be working with." I followed him in a poky little kitchen which had a fridge, a few cupboards, a kettle and a microwave in it. He opened the fridge and said, "I'll get the others to sort out a space for you." Inside I saw little piles of food, all neatly labelled with the owners' names. It was the same with the cupboards. This gave me my first pangs of doubt as to whether I'd done the right thing by coming here. An integral part of station life, is the mess; it's the heart of the watch and it suddenly dawned on me that I wasn't on a watch or a fire station, now, and there was no mess here. It didn't feel right. "Right, let's go to the main office. I'll introduce you to some of the blokes and show you where you'll be sitting." I followed along behind him, still carrying my bag full of clothes, towel and washing gear.

There was a big long desk facing a wall, with shelves full up with folders. I was shown to the space that I'd be occupying. I wouldn't even be getting my own desk! The ADO gave me the world's thickest folder and said, "Start reading that, Steve, it's as good a place to start as any." and left me to it. There were two other blokes sitting at the desk and I recognised them immediately. They had been firemen on another watch at my station and were younger than me. Both were wearing white shirts and Sub Officer rank markings, having been bumped up two ranks from fireman. On station, the only people who wear white shirts are substantive Station Officers and above. Even temporary Stn O's acting up have to wear blue shirts, along with the rest of us underlings. They both looked up, looking a bit surprised. "You here on light duties mate?" one of them asked. "No, I'm detached in to see if I like it, then, if I do, I might be staying." I said. They looked at each other and grinned. "We didn't ever expect to see you here, Steve. Wouldn't have thought it was your cup of tea?" I grinned back and said, "Stn O wages, no nights or weekends and early finishes is definitely my cup of tea! What time do you usually get away?" Their reply brought me back down to earth with a bump. "About half past four, usually." I thought they were winding me up and laughed, "Fuck off, I was told that I'd home by dinner time every day!" Then it was their turn to laugh. "That was back in the old days, mate. It doesn't happen now. You have to sign in and out of the office and if you sign out before half four, questions are asked. One or two of the old boys still get away with doing their paperwork at home, but that's only because they've been doing it for years and no one want's to tell them that they can't." That wasn't what I wanted to hear, but I thought they were misleading me and, as had become the norm, I started over thinking things. Perhaps they didn't want me there because I out ranked them? If I stayed, I'd get the Stn O's position that they were hoping for. I grinned at them and started to read the huge folder that had been put in front of me.

This folder was full of information, but I couldn't retain any of it because it was so boring. I was reading the same paragraph over and over again, but it just wasn't going in. What didn't help was that my brain was going at 100 mph, trying to make sense of what I'd just been told. After about an hour, which felt like two, another fire safety officer came over and asked if I'd like to go with him to do an inspection. I was on my feet with my jacket on before he'd finished speaking; anything to get away from that folder. He drove us to an address in Forest Gate where, apparently, he'd been several times before. It was a big house that the owner had converted into four or five bedsits, which was quite common in that area at the time. The outside of the building looked run down and dirty, the small front garden was overgrown. When the owner let us in, I was genuinely shocked at the state of the place. It was filthy and in a state of disrepair, with plaster falling from the damp walls in places and black mould visible on what remained. The first room we went into was the communal kitchen which, again, was filthy. The fire safety officer asked the owner why he hadn't rectified any of the issues that he had highlighted on previous visits, only to be met with a weak grin and, "Not understand the English language". The officer kept his cool and said, "But we've written to you several times, in your own language, as well as English, telling you what needs to be done and to get someone who can understand to act as an interpreter, if you can't speak English." The owner just shrugged and gave the same weak grin. I was fuming and struggled to keep my mouth shut. This was a rogue landlord of the worst kind, charging unfortunate people a lot of rent money and not spending any of it on their welfare or safety. And, in my opinion, he could understand English perfectly well when it suited him. The officer wrote some notes and we left. When we got back in his car, I looked at him and said, "I don't know how you stayed so patient with him? You were even calling him, Sir, when the bloke is a total scum bag!" He looked at me and said, "I know how you feel, Steve. I've been into plenty of fires and seen the burnt bodies, the same as you have. It angers me just as much, but there's a process that has to be followed and, eventually, other authorities will get involved. It takes a while, but these people do get shut down and, when they do, that's one less death trap for us all to deal with." I completely understood what he was saying; I just doubted that I could treat such low life with as much respect. It was certainly an eye opener.

If we attended a fire in a HMO, (house of multiple occupancy), there would almost always be serious breaches of fire safety regulations exposed in the aftermath. But we just used to request the attendance of a fire safety officer and leave it for them to sort out. We never gave it a second thought once we left the job. When we got back to the dingy office, I sat staring at the blank pages of my giant fire safety folder for another couple of hours.

A bit later in the day, another fire safety officer came and asked me if I'd like to come with him on his afternoon inspection. He said, "It's Romford, on your way home, so follow me in your own car and when we're done, you can go straight home and I'll sign you out when I leave the office later." Of course, I jumped at the chance. I sneaked by bag out of the office and threw it in my car, then followed the chap to what looked like a disused social club, not far from the Greyhound Stadium. The place had been derelict for some time and wasn't secure, so we had no problem gaining access. Someone, quite rightly, had reported the building as a fire risk to the local station and they had passed it on to fire safety after their initial visit. The file on the premises was old and out of date. The phone numbers for the owners were all obsolete, so I got the impression that the place had changed hands at least once before being abandoned and was just waiting to be torched so that something else could be built on the land it occupied. Over thinking again? Maybe - but I think it was more fireman's instinct. We did a thorough search of the building for tramps, or anyone else who might be living in there, then looked for any obvious dangers to any fire crews that might be committed if the place went up. If we had found anything, the details would be added to the Brigade's CRR, (central risk register), system and would be mentioned on any call slips for shouts to the address. We didn't find anything and I remember thinking that it would be a fun job to attend if it did go up. The officer was busy taking notes the whole time. When we were done, I asked, "What happens now?" He looked at me and shrugged, "Well, first, we've got to find out who actually owns the building, which might be difficult because they obviously don't want to be found. Then, if we find them, the process of getting them to make the premises safe and secure can begin. But it's going to be a long drawn out process. Nothing happens quickly in fire safety." Which is complete opposite of the operational firefighting that I was used to; where everything happens very quickly. I jumped in my car and drove home, but my head was spinning for the whole journey. I kept thinking that I'd made a mistake and fire safety wasn't for me after all. But how would I get out of it now? Two senior officers had pulled strings to get me there and I didn't want to let them both down.

I got up earlier the next morning and decided to give it a proper go before making my mind up. On the way there, I thought of all the positives that had made me go there in the first place. By the time I pulled into the yard, I was full of enthusiasm again. I made myself a coffee and settled down in front of the dreaded folder again, trying my best to actually understand and make sense of what it was I was reading. After an hour or so, the ADO came in to see how I was getting on. All I could think of saying was, "It's heavy going Guv, isn't it." pointing to the folder and laughed. He nodded and said, "OK, have a break from it for a while. I'll take you over to the filing rooms to show you what we do over there. You'll be spending a lot of time in there initially, as you're new." I followed him down the stairs and across East Ham's drill yard to a dingy looking building sitting over in one corner. Inside was just as dingy as the outside, with rows and rows of tall filing cabinets. Out of the gloom came a fireman that I recognised from another station and before the ADO could introduce us, we had greeted each other with a hand shake. The bloke had been in fire safety on light duties for a long time and had spent most of his time there in the depths of the filing department. You don't have to be away from fire stations for long to be forgotten and seeing him took me a bit by surprise. "You here on light duties, too, Steve?" he asked. The ADO piped up and said, "No, he started here yesterday and I want you to show him how things work in our filing system." He then turned on his heels and left us to it. I felt depressed straight away. There was almost no natural light in the building and there were files and paperwork, which I'd always hated, stacked from floor to ceiling. We sat on a box of files and had a catch up for a while, then the other fireman said, "Oh well, I suppose I'd better start showing you what we have to do. It's a doddle and you're out of the way over here." I looked up at all the filing cabinets surrounding us and said, "Don't bother showing me anything mate, I won't be staying." My mind was made up now; this wasn't for me. We sat and chatted for a while then I took myself back up to the office. I had decided that the folder was the lesser of two evils compared to the filing. A short while later, one of the jumped up firemen from my station asked if I wanted to accompany him on his next visit. Grateful for any excuse to get out, I said yes. He took me to an industrial park in the arse end of Rainham, (on the extreme eastern edge of London's ground), where we had to inspect various business units in a huge two story building. Gaining entry proved difficult because the business owners knew there were serious breaches of fire safety regulations and no one wanted to let us in. When we finally got in, we saw for ourselves that there were serious issues. A few of the people who were employed by some of the businesses approached us quietly and expressed their concerns, but were too afraid to raise them with their employers. The employers themselves were evasive at best. Each business had a folder and in each folder, the contact details for the owner of the building, were different. Eventually, after making notes of all the contraventions, we left having achieved not a great deal. In the car on the way back to the office, I said to the fireman, "You know all those business owners were taking the piss out of us, don't you?" He gave me a puzzled look so I followed up. "They all pay their rent to someone and they must know who that is. So why can't they tell us who owns the building?" It was the same old story. The landlord didn't want to spend any money to make the workers safe and the business owners didn't want to be inconvenienced with stopped or delayed production while work was carried out to rectify the problems. The fireman, in his white shirt and rank markings, just shrugged his shoulders and said, "Well, we've done our bit for today. We'll go back in another couple of months' time to see if anything's been done." I'd heard enough now. What if there was a big fire in that building today, tomorrow, or next week and people were injured or killed? I joined the job to fight fires and save people when necessary, not to stand back and keep my fingers crossed. The fire safety blokes were doing their job to the best of their ability, but it was too frustrating for me.

When we got back to East Ham I went straight to the ADO's office. "Guv, sorry, but I want to go back to my station." He looked up and said, "Oh, you need to pick some of your stuff up from your locker? No problem. When you get back I'll go through the signing in and out procedure with you and introduce you to some of the girls who work alongside us." I was a bit embarrassed, but stuck to my guns. "No Guv, I mean I want to go back to my station and stay there. This isn't for me, I'm sorry. I appreciate you giving me this opportunity, but I don't want to waste any more of your time than I already have." He gave me a look of half disbelief and said, "OK, it's not for everyone, thanks for being upfront. I'll make the call. For the rest of today, just make yourself busy in the filing building." We shook hands and I went downstairs to the yard. As I got there, the station bells went down and East Ham's pump ladder tipped out on the bell. I wished I was going with them and knew there and then that I'd made the right decision. Instead of going into the filing building, I got in my car and drove home. I was determined to get home by dinner time at least once during my stint in fire safety! I had lasted a day and a half, which I think is probably some sort of record. My first day in fire safety was my watch's second day duty of the tour. My second day there would have been their first night. I reported for duty on our second night. So, out of a tour of two days and two nights, I'd completed the first day on a fire station and was back for the second night. When I went into the watchroom, just before the change of watch, the day watch were in there along with my own. A couple of my blokes looked at me and said, "What you doing here?" There was no escaping the stick I was going to get, so I just came out with it. "Fire safety isn't for me. Fuck that." There were a few seconds of silence, then the watchroom erupted with laughter and then the typical fireman's smart arse comments came thick and fast. "At least you gave it a good go, though, mate" "What, did you get too sunburnt in your garden?" "Where are your Stn O rank markings?" "Have they chucked you out already?" It was wonderful and I knew then that I would spend the rest of my career on a fire station, because that's where I belonged. I'd just have to deal with any shit from above the best I could and hope that I made it to retirement before doing something that would get me the sack. I would have to tread a very treacherous path, though, in my remaining years.

CHAPTER 11.

The retained

In London, everyone who lives or works there has the luxury of being covered by a full time fire brigade, or 'wholetime', as it is known. That is, there are lots of fire stations throughout the city and they are manned twenty four hours a day, seven days a week, three hundred and sixty days a year. Call 999 in London and you could expect a fire engine, or two, or three, to turn up at your address within minutes and the firemen who arrived at your emergency, no matter how big or small, would be professionals. They would have been trained professionally throughout their careers and attended emergency calls on a daily basis. We were the real deal, as it were. Unfortunately, not everyone in the UK benefits from this level of protection. Big cities, (other than London), and counties, employ professional wholetime firefighters in their most densely populated areas, but use retained firefighters, (part time volunteers), in the lesser populated areas. Some counties and shires don't employ any professional firemen at all. Instead, they rely entirely on volunteers. To make things clear, the people who volunteer to provide fire cover in their local community don't really have a choice. If they didn't volunteer, there wouldn't be any fire cover where they live. Retained fire stations sit empty until an emergency call comes in and, when it does, the volunteers respond to pagers and make their way from home, or work, to the fire station in order to attend whatever emergency they've been called to. Shop keepers, mechanics, postmen, builders, school teachers, etc, undergo a short period of initial basic training, then have to attend a drill night at their local station for a few hours each week to develop their skills. This, in my opinion, is a total cop out on the government's part. (Even Trumpton and Pontypandy were wholetime!) I think that everyone should be covered by a professional fire service, no matter where they live; just the same as they have access to a professional police service, ambulance service, hospital and GP surgery. As I write this, I can imagine lots of retained firefighters spitting feathers as they read my words, because I know that a lot of them consider themselves to be professional. It is not my intention to insult anyone, but the fact is, they aren't. By definition, a profession is something that someone does for a living. It's impossible to perform at the same level as a wholetime fireman if you only do the job occasionally, no matter how good your intentions are. That said, they do their best and serve a purpose. Unfortunately, that purpose is, largely, to plug the gaps left by politicians. It's a no win situation for the local communities and the volunteers who serve them, many of whom could become wholetime firefighters if they didn't volunteer because politicians would then have to provide some sort of wholetime cover in their area. They're damned if they do and damned if they don't.

Historically, there hasn't been any love lost between wholetime and retained firemen. This isn't just because of our professional differences; it goes a lot deeper than that. Unfortunately, over the years, there have been more than a few disputes between various brigades and the government, local and national. Most of these disputes have been about cuts to the service, ie, removal of appliances and closure of stations. Some of them have lead to strikes, which is always a last resort but sometimes necessary, usually resulting in some sort of compromise. Something that sticks in the throat of most wholetime firemen and union members is, the vast majority of retained volunteers carry on working and provide fire cover in their areas. It doesn't matter what quality of fire cover they provide because the governments can tell the public that they are providing it and keeping everyone safe. Their actions just undermine the efforts of the wholetime in trying to maintain the level of service that they feel the public deserves, which is something that doesn't affect them, or their local communities, because they have nothing to lose. They are already operating on a bare bones volunteer service. One of the stations that I served at was close to the border with Essex. Occasionally, we'd be ordered onto Essex Fire Brigade ground to cover something that they couldn't. I remember one time when Essex were in dispute with their local government about cuts to the service and took strike action to fight against the loss of appliances. We knew that we would be called over the border more often during their strike but our national Fire Brigades Union were fine with that, as long as we didn't work with the retained strike breakers. We are trained to different standards and it was deemed dangerous for us to work alongside them. The LFB agreed and that was that. One day, early in the strike, we picked up a fire in a property just over the border. My machine and one other London machine were ordered. About 20 minutes after our arrival, when everything was already under control, an Essex machine turned up. The crew got off and started trying to join in, using our hose reels and cutting away gear! One of them picked up a hose reel that was next to me and started to damp down the extinguished fire. I looked at him and said, "What you doing here, I thought you were on strike?" "No, we're not on strike", he replied. So I said, "Well the proper firemen are on strike in Essex today", which he didn't like. "What do you mean proper firemen? We are proper firemen", he said, looking quite indignant. "No you're not mate, your retained, so, put that hose reel down and fuck off!" He put the hose reel down and stood there, dumb struck. Just then, his officer in charge came over with his shiny white helmet and asked what was going on. He was closely followed by the bloke in charge of the other London machine in attendance, who said to the white hat, "We don't work with you, so round your boys up, get back on your machine and fuck off". The Essex retained man in charge turned away, muttering, and off they fucked. Apparently, he put in a complaint against us with an Essex senior officer, who then complained to a London senior officer, but nothing came of it. We were just made aware of it.

One night, while serving at the same station, we were called to a four pump fire across the border. From the call slip, I saw that it was quite a well known pub and restaurant alight. Three Essex machines had been mobilised and us, the only London machine, to complete the attendance. I knew the pub and it was a big, very old, building. I remember thinking at the time that wouldn't last long if the fire had got hold. It took us while to get there and as we approached the pub we could see plenty of smoke, but not much in the way of flames. Two of the retained Essex appliances were already in attendance, had got to work and were busy squirting water onto the roof, which did its job perfectly and prevented any water from getting inside the building. We parked our machine up a little way back from the other appliances, which served two purposes. First, it didn't hinder access for any additional appliances that might be ordered and kept the fireground clear. Second, we didn't want to use any of our gear, which is always a nightmare to get back after a job, allowing us to get away quickly once the fire was under control. We dismounted and went to report to the Officer in charge, who seemed a bit flustered. "Right", he said, "You lot get BA on and go to the other end of the building. Enter through the door that end, go up the stairs and see if the fire has spread to that end of the roof". I managed to contain the grin that was trying to spread across my face and, trying to look concerned, said, "I can't do that mate". Now he looked even more flustered and a bit angry, too. "I'm ordering you to take your crew and ent...." I cut him off abrubtly. "I still can't do it mate and I'm not going to. One, there's no way we're entering a burning building without water - and you haven't got any laid on at that end – and two, if you want us to rig in BA, I'm going to have to order on more London machines. (London and Essex BA entry control boards, sets and procedures aren't the same and you can't mix and match). "In other words, I'm going to have to make up your job for you". At this point, he looked like he was going to explode with rage, so to calm him down I said, "Is there anything else you want us to do?" I could see that he just wanted to punch me, which tickled me even more, but he was wrong and I was right. End of. He threw his toys out of the pram and shouted, "If you're not going to do as I tell you, you might as well go and sit back on your machine!" "OK mate", I said, as I turned and went back to my crew. "Our brief is to go and sit back on the machine boys. I'll try to get us away as quick as I can." As we were walking back to our appliance, the third Essex machine arrived and pulled up behind our pump Ladder. (Geography dictated that we'd sometimes beat certain Essex stations onto their own ground). These were wholetime Essex firemen who we knew. We'd worked and trained together plenty of times and, unlike their retained brethren, we'd supported them when they were on strike. We had a good rapport. I recounted the conversation I'd just had to the two crews, who found it just as amusing as I had, then we went and did as we were told and they went to meet the OIC. As we sat watching events unfold through the windows of our appliance, it became clear that the wholetime Stn O had taken over the job and was now running things. The jets that had been aimed at the smoke issuing from the roof had now been taken inside the building by BA crews. The colour of the smoke started to change and it was obvious that progress was being made. We all made the decision to ignore our previous orders, as the OIC who had told us to fuck off was no longer in charge, went to help our wholetime Essex mates and colleagues. I spoke with their Stn O and said, "We don't want or need any more machines on this so, if you don't mind, we'll get stuck in and help where and however we can." He was happy with this and we did indeed get stuck in. By now, it was apparent that the fire was on the first floor of building, not in the roof as the previous OIC had assumed. It could have been on the ground floor and the smoke would still have issued from the roof. It's the highest part of the building and smoke rises! When the first wholetime Essex BA crew came out, I stood with their Stn O and listened to their debrief. There was no fire on the ground floor, they had extinguished the staircase to the first floor but were hampered by a hefty locked door which prevented them from entering the fire compartment. I decided to take my crew inside the grand old building on the ground floor to start doing some salvage work, sheeting up to prevent things from becoming water damaged, etc. Not the most glamorous job, but an essential part of firefighting. While we were sheeting up, a retained BA crew came in to relieve to first crew, but didn't make any progress beyond the staircase. Again, I listened to their debrief to the OIC when they came out and thought they sounded rattled by the experience. From what we'd learnt from the BA crews, my crew and I knew exactly where the fire was and agreed that the best tactic was to pull down what remained of the ceiling above us and fight the fire from below to stop it from spreading, while waiting for the next BA crew to enter. We picked up one of the jets that had been abandoned outside and some ceiling hooks and axes from the Essex machines, then set about pulling the ceiling down from the cover of doorways. As soon as we made a hole, we could see flames. It really was play time. The bigger the hole became, the more fire we saw and the more we extinguished. It was great fun. We were working in clear air, so didn't need BA, which is always a good experience. After a while, we'd done what we could from the ground floor and decided to try to tackle the hefty door into the fire compartment that no one had managed to breach yet. We went to the first floor externally, via a 9 metre ladder, and set up our jet on a flat roof adjacent to the door, ready for our entrance. By now, the fire was all but beat, but there were still pockets of fire that needed putting out. We had been joined now by some of our wholetime Essex mates, who had also decided to dump their sets and join in the fun. When we got to the flat roof, there was a group of very young firefighters on there, doing their best to gain entry to the fire compartment. These were retained, but they were good lads. They were working hard and they were determined. I walked across the flat roof to speak to them and ask what difficulties they were encountering. As I did, I could feel the roof going floppy and saggy under my feet. I crouched down beside them and said, "I think we need to get off here fellas, the roofs gone." They were tucked away in a corner, (good safe firefighting tactics), and hadn't noticed the roof sagging. They looked at me as I showed them the roof bending under my weight, without venturing too far into the middle, and then followed me to safety. It brought back memories of myself, learning from older, experienced hands and I spent the next hour working with these young, keen firemen. Each of them were eager to listen, look and learn; and would have made excellent wholetime firemen. I sincerely hope some of them took that path. From what could have been a disastrous job, initially, it turned into one of the most enjoyable I experienced. Mostly, because of those retained youngsters. Hats off to you lads!

CHAPTER 12.

Bonfire night.

November the 5th was traditionally the busiest night of the year for Firemen all over the country, especially those that worked in large, heavily populated cities. With so many gardens in close proximity to each other, each hosting its own home firework display and bonfire, it was inevitable that there would be many bonfires getting out of control and setting fire to other things, like sheds, fences and even houses. Then there were stray fireworks, lit by well-meaning but incompetent parents - as well as irresponsible adults showing off to their mates with the biggest, most expensive fireworks they could buy. Usually, these were professional display grade rockets and bombs that were bought illegally from one of the fly by night firework shops that used to pop up every year for a few weeks before disappearing again. In London, we used to implement what was called bonfire night procedure. All but the most essential routines were abandoned, you eat as and when you can and, if there was enough personnel on duty, the mess manager would come off the run so he could keep us all supplied with hot food and drinks, should we manage to make it back to the station for a short time during the night. We would be batch mobilised by control, which meant that instead of getting one shout at a time, we would be sent a list of incidents to attend on a very long call slip. We would work through the list, one by one, and when we'd taken care of all the calls, would book mobile and available by RT, (Radio Telephone). Sometimes, we'd get mobilised to another incident straight away, sometimes we'd be told to go back to the station to get another batch of shouts that they were sending over on the tele-printer, sometimes we'd make it all the way back to the station and get the opportunity to get something to eat. Those occasions were a bit tense, as we drove back listening to all other call signs being mobilised over the radio and just waiting, expecting our own call sign to be next. The would always be a smattering of four and six pump fires in the area, too, which would tie up resources and make the rest of us busier, covering other stations' grounds. Then, just as suddenly as the chaos had started, it would end, almost like someone had flicked off a switch.

I will always remember my first bonfire night. I was obviously still in my first year and based at a very busy East London station. Listening to the old hands talking about all the house jobs, fours and sixes they'd had in the past on this night, got my juices going. I couldn't wait. When the night came, I was ordered out to stand by at Bethnal Green. I was gutted that I wouldn't be spending it with my own watch, but they assured me that I'd be just as busy there as at my own station. I'd stood by there a few times before and it was a good watch. Nice blokes, good firemen and a great mess manager. It was always good entertainment when I stood by there. There were some real characters on the watch and they always had me in stitches. The watchroom was full when I arrived. The mayhem hadn't started properly yet and they were waiting for my arrival so they could put the pump on the run. "Alright, Steve? Test your set and get your bed down now, mate, while you've got a chance. Grab a quick cuppa if you can, Mick's up there with a pot on the go." With that, the bells went down and their Pump ladder was called out to the first shout of the evening. I chucked my gear on the back of the pump, tested my set quickly and it went on the run before I had finished filling my log book in. Once we were good to go, I went upstairs with my bedding under my arm, found a spare bed in the dorm and made it up. Then I walked into the mess, where I was handed a fresh cup of fire brigade tea by Mick the mess manager. "When the ladder gets back mate, I'll be jumping across so I can spend more time here, keeping you lot fed and watered", he laughed. "Only Spag Bol tonight I'm afraid, Steve. It's quick and easy to heat up, as and when we get a chance to eat." I got to drink half of my tea before the bells went down again. We hadn't been batch mobilised, so it was just a normal fire call to a bonfire out of control. Sometimes, the bonfire wouldn't be out of control at all, it would just be a miserable neighbour or busy body who didn't like to see people enjoying themselves. In these cases, we'd have a look and make sure the fire wasn't at risk of spreading, then tell the revellers to have some water standing by, just in case. If it was dangerous, or out of control, we'd either put it out or just knock it down a bit.

My night at Bethnal Green was a busy one. The pump had 19 shouts in all, including the couple of batch mobilisation lists we received. They weren't all local, either. We covered a wide area, because lots of stations were tied up and busy, even going onto Western Command's area a couple of times. Included in these shouts were two 'rescues' that I was involved with, even though, at the time, I didn't consider them to be rescues. One was on Whitechapel's ground. It was a shop with a flat above it and someone had torched the doorway to the shop, cutting off the flat's occupants' only means of escape. They weren't in immediate danger, but were panicking and hanging out of the front widow. Not knowing whether the fire had breached the shop doorway and seeing people hanging out of the window, frightened and screaming, we pitched a ladder to the window. I was a guest that night, so I didn't rush to steal the hosereel branch; instead, leaving it to the fireman I was riding alongside. As he set about extinguishing the fire, I went up the ladder to check out the flat and reassure the people inside. There was a language problem, so I couldn't explain that there was no immediate danger to them, but they didn't calm down and wanted me to do something. One of them started to climb out of the window, trying to get onto the ladder. I pulled him back inside, got on the ladder myself, then got him out of the window onto the ladder safely and walked him down. No great shakes, it was only a first floor window; then I went back up for his Mrs, who he had completely abandoned! Same drill, except by the time we got to ground level, the fire was out and it was all done and dusted. I felt a bit embarrassed, if I'm honest, because I had got the people out of the window and down the ladder when, if they had waited a few minutes, they could have walked down the staircase and through the shop to the street. Bearing in mind that I was still a buck with less than a year in the job, I thought that Bethnal Green's blokes would have taken the piss. Instead, I got a "Well done mate." And off we went to the next shout. The second one was on either Shoreditch's or Clerkenwell's ground, I can't remember now. There had been a fire in a maisonette and we weren't the first machine there. When we arrived, the fire was out and the initial BA crew were just starting their secondary search of the property. The smoke wasn't that heavy, so I went in to give them a hand without BA. In the first bedroom I checked was a young child, about two years old, I'd guess, asleep in a cot. I picked her up and started to make my way out. As I did, I passed the BA crew on their way upstairs to search. I think they brought a further two children out, from memory. The fire had been small and was extinguished quickly, so the smoke logging wasn't that heavy and, with the bedroom doors shut, the kids hadn't suffered at all from smoke inhalation. They were just a bit bewildered. The parents had, apparently, left them at home alone while they went to a firework party! Again, I didn't consider this to be a rescue, because it wasn't a desperate life or death situation. So we left it with the home station's crew, booked mobile and off we went to the next shout. Suddenly, there were no more shouts. When we booked mobile for the last time that night, about midnight, the radio stayed silent all the way back to the station. There was nothing on the tele-printer, either, so we made our way upstairs to the mess, where we caught up with the pump ladder's crew. They'd been tied up at a six pump fire for most of the night and had only just got back themselves. Within 20 minutes, we were all eating hot food and drinking tea, finally falling into our beds at around 01:30 hrs. The next night, I was at my own station and was keen to hear about what they'd picked up the night before. When I walked into the watchroom, my watch asked, "Well? Did you have a good night? And all started laughing. "Two recues in one night, well done mate." I was surprised to say the least. "What are you talking about? We didn't rescue anyone last night?" Then my Governor piped up and said, "It's all on the morning summary, Steve. We saw that the Green's pump had a couple of persons reported last night, so we knew you'd have been there, but I had a call early this morning from their Governor, telling what you did and how well you'd done." I still don't consider these incident's as rescues because, in my eyes, they weren't life or death situations. Life or death rescues would come later in my career.

Over the years, one bonfire night merged another, but there are still a few that stick in my mind; one which fell on a dry Saturday night. I was riding in charge of the pump, as usual. As it was a weekend and no one had to wait to get home from work before starting the festivities, the shouts started coming in thick and fast, right from the start of my night shift. It was expected to be a very busy night at a very busy station so, in his wisdom, our DO, (Divisional Officer), had invited the local press to ride with him in his fire brigade car to report on the night events. The idea was, they would sit in a strategic position listening to the brigade radio in his car and, if something interesting came over the airwaves, he would drive them to the incident on the bell. As anticipated, it turned into a very busy night. Our pump attended two four pump fires on other stations' grounds and a small house fire that turned out to be a fatal; as well as all the other, usual, bonfire night stuff. One call we attended was to a bonfire out of control on a rundown estate of flats in Plaistow. When we pulled into estate, we could see a huge bonfire that the locals had built in the middle of the road. There were kids playing all around it and their parents were leaning on their balconies, watching the fun and games. Then we turned up - the spoil sports. Immediately, the atmosphere changed from one of joy, to one of hostility. Before we had even dismounted the machine, we started getting verbal abuse from the kids. Then the missiles started raining in. Stones, bricks, bottles and anything else they could get their grubby hands on. We got off to have a look and a word with the 'responsible adult' in charge of the fire, just to assure them that we wouldn't spoil their fun unless it was causing a danger to life or property. Then the adults joined in with the abuse and threats of violence. I'd already seen enough and decided that the fire wouldn't present any danger to anyone, unless one of the kids fell on it, and we started making our way back to the machine to leave. Then the first of the rockets was fired at us at knee height, just missing us by a couple of feet. It wasn't our ground, so we hadn't known what to expect, but when we spoke to the home watch about it later that night when we met at another job, they laughed and said, "We won't drive onto that estate on bonfire night without a police escort. It's the same every year." In other words, we don't go there, because a police escort on any night is almost impossible, but on bonfire night, it's not going to happen. Whenever we left estates like that, with kids running around, we had to have two firemen hanging on the ladders on the back of the appliance as we drove out to stop the kids from jumping on them to get a ride. There would always be one kid trying to hang on longer than all his mates, to the point of putting his life at risk, but no one on the appliance would be able to see them as we drove off. Hence two firemen hanging off the ladders until we were well out of the way, usually being hounded by kids as we went.

The rest of that night passed much as any other – busy beyond anything normal then suddenly quiet. The thing is, when it goes quiet, you don't know if it's over for the night, or whether it's just a lull. This particular night, when we finally got back to the station, the DO's car was parked on the forecourt. We hadn't seen him or the local media all night and I'd completely forgotten that they were supposed to be shadowing us. We went upstairs to the mess to grab a hot drink and, if we were lucky, something to eat. Two of the lads didn't even take their firegear off before going up, because they thought we'd be straight back out again. When we got to the mess, it was empty. The pump ladder was out on a fire call. We each got a hot drink and, thankfully, the ladders crew had left our basic dinner in the hot plate. It was baked to death, but we were just grateful to get some food in our stomachs. Just as we sat down to shovel as much in as we could before the bells went down again, the DO appeared. "Steve, could you get a couple of your blokes to go downstairs and rig in BA? The reporter wants some pictures of firemen in BA for the papers." I couldn't believe what I was hearing and looked for a giveaway smile to start appearing on his face, but he was serious! I looked at him for a second and said, "Well, the journalists can go fuck themselves then! We've been out all night, through all sorts of shit, the blokes are all tired and hungry and I'm not going to ask them to pose for photos. Sorry, the local press will have to wait until we've eaten then, if we haven't been called out again by then, maybe a couple of my crew will agree to being photographed." I was fuming! Then, he waved the red flag and said, "But they're tired and want to go home now, so come on, get a couple of blokes down there." I stared at him with pure contempt in my eyes. "Well, I'm not going to tell anyone to do that. I fact, I'm not even going to ask them nicely. If you want them to do it, you're going to have to order them – and, if they refuse, I'm, going to be on their side." then turned and walked away from him. Unfortunately, two of my blokes did as he asked them and the journalist got her photos. Whether they wanted their five minutes of fame, or felt threatened by the senior officer, I don't know. But before they went downstairs, I said to them, "You know you don't have to do this. It's your choice, but you don't have to do it and if you refuse, I'm going to back you up." The thing I couldn't understand was, it had been a very busy night and we'd attended all sorts of interesting jobs and worked hard. How come we hadn't seen the DO with his entourage all night? The answer, when it came, didn't surprise me. Apparently, the DO was glory hunting and they spent all night chasing what he thought were going to be big fires. The journalists were given a nice tour of London all night without actually seeing a flame, while we were working our bollocks off in the area that they should have been reporting on!

My second station was in an area with a very diverse population, mostly Asian, so bonfire night was gradually overshadowed by Diwali and other religious festivities, all of which the locals would celebrate with fireworks. The Asians didn't care too much for bonfires, but they loved a firework! The bigger and louder the better! We attended some great firework parties on these nights when someone would put a call in, usually a concerned neighbour. We would turn up to have a look and, straight away, be offered food from the fantastic spreads they used to put on. The people were happy and there was often no booze involved, depending what religious festival was being celebrated, so there was no drunken or abusive behaviour. Of course, we had to stay a while to make sure everything was safe and to embrace the diverse community we served by eating the food they offered us. It was delicious! Even with no bonfires, the fireworks still kept us busy and we picked up plenty of jobs caused by them. But fireworks didn't stop with bonfire night and religious celebrations; as they became more readily available throughout the year, people would find any excuse to have a display at home. New Year's Eve, when I was a kid, was celebrated by everyone opening their doors at midnight, standing on the door step banging saucepans together and wishing the neighbours a happy new year. Not so now. It's a firework fest that goes on into the small hours, the same as Christmas Eve, Halloween, Birthdays and any number of other reasons that people can dream up as an excuse to set fire to vast amounts of money, while causing distress and mayhem outside of their little bubble. I've seen dogs and other animals absolutely terrified by the very loud fireworks that are now available to the general public – and it's not just for one night a year any more. I have friends who have lost Horses because they've gone down with colic as a result of being petrified by fireworks. I've spent hours, off duty, at livery yards, to keep an eye on the horses and hoping that a stray firework doesn't come down in a hay barn, or a stable full of straw. It's the same with the Chinese lanterns that seem to have become popular now. How on earth it is still legal to send a vessel filled with flammable liquid into the air, suspended by nothing more than a paper balloon, I don't know. Again, the damage and the horrific injuries to animals they sometimes cause, is an outrage in my eyes. Picture this; a horse asleep in a field has a Chinese lantern land on it. It is wearing rug made of nylon, which is then doused in paraffin and ignited. The horse is strapped into the rug and can't get away, so the nylon melts and burns the hair and skin of the poor creature, which then dies a horrible death. This happens more often than you would believe. In my opinion, having seen the bad side of fireworks, etc, from a professional point of view, as well as personal, they should be banned from public use and restricted to organised displays only, where there will be proper safety measures in place.

CHAPTER 13.
Battle of the sexes

This is another very sensitive subject and one that is quite controversial, but I've been asked so many times, by so many people - should women become firefighters? – That I'd be dodging the issue if I omitted mention of it altogether. I've never been one to side step difficult subjects or controversy, so I'm going to give my own honest opinion and highlight some of the events that have shaped my thinking. I'll start by saying that the question shouldn't be *should* women become firefighters, but *can* women become firefighters. It's no one's place to say what a woman, or a man come to that, should and shouldn't do as a job. But we are all entitled to an opinion on whether they can be effective in that role, especially if it's based on personal experience. Unfortunately, there isn't a definitive answer. If a woman can meet the same selection criteria as men do to get in the brigade, then pass all the same tests during training, there is no reason why they shouldn't, or can't, pass out of training school as effective firefighters. Being totally honest, I've worked alongside some excellent female firefighters. I've also worked alongside some who should never have been allowed to set foot on the fireground.

My first experience of females in the job was back when I was at training school. There were two female recruits there at the time I did my basic training and all the rest were male. Neither of them was in my squad, but everyone saw how polar opposite they were to each other. One of them had passed the selection process, including the fitness test and medical, but once at training school it became very apparent to everyone that she just couldn't do the job. Even basic things like running out and rolling up lengths of hose were beyond her capability. The trainers at Southwark were at a loss what to do with her, so she was placed on light duties and they would take it in turns working with her during their lunch breaks to try to help her with fitness, strength and weight loss. In the whole 20 weeks that I was there doing my recruit training, she didn't take part in one single drill and was still there when my squad passed out as qualified firefighters. She was a lovely person and was liked by everyone, but there is no way that she was going to make it as a firefighter. In fact, I don't know what was going through her mind when she applied. But, whatever happened wasn't really her fault. Someone had seen fit to pass her on her fitness test and, possibly, turned a blind eye to her medical results during the selection process. The last I heard was that she had become pregnant and was given a job in the offices somewhere.

The other female recruit was as good as any of the male recruits there. She excelled at training school and didn't duck out of anything, even the tasks we used to have to do that have since been scrapped because they were deemed too difficult for females to do. The pick up and carry was one such task and had to be completed as part of our intermediate tests and assessments. Basically, an Ogle dummy, (crash test dummy), dressed in full firegear, was placed in a prone position in the middle of a room. Then we would have to manoeuvre the dummy to a wall, where we would then get it onto its knees, then lift and thrust it into the wall and hold it in a standing position. Once it was standing, we would shove our shoulder into its midriff and pick it up in a fireman's carry. It would then be carried a certain distance before being lowered carefully to the ground and put in the recovery position. An Ogle dummy is, or was, filled with sand and weighed twelve stone dry. The ones we used were saturated, because of all the water that we used to squirt around, and weighed quite a bit more than that. Plus, the saturated firegear it was dressed in must have weighed another couple of stone. All recruits had to do this unaided and were marked on it. It was to simulate a situation where you might have to get your BA partner out of a fire if they went down, or to get an unconscious casualty out of a building. If anyone failed, they didn't progress with their training. It was extremely difficult because the dummy behaved just like a real unconscious casualty; a dead weight. I actually sustained quite a severe groin strain when I was tested on it and had to dose myself up with pain killers for about a week afterwards in order to carry on with my training. But this particular female recruit passed test with flying colours, proving that she was as good and as strong as any male in training centre at the time. In fact, when we used to watch her squad doing drills, you couldn't pick her out from the rest of them when she was dressed in her firegear. The other task that we had to complete that has now been scrapped was the carry down. We would have to pick up a live casualty from the mezzanine floor on the third floor of the drill tower and get them into a fireman's carry. Then, climb over the balcony and onto a 135ladder, carry them down the ladder to ground level, then put them down in the same controlled manner as we'd learnt with the dummies. Again, a very hard task, but one that she completed without any problem. I understand that she went on to complete a very successful career in the London Fire Brigade.

I spent most of my career on all male watch, but saw out my last few years with two female firefighters on my watch. Once again, they were both lovely people but polar opposites when it came to ability and attitude. One had struggled at training school but eventually passed out to join an operational watch. She seemed keen enough, but didn't possess the necessary attention span that is required if you are to be an effective firefighter. Trying to teach her things was an ordeal because you could spend an hour showing her something until she perfected it, but by the next day she's had completely forgotten how to do it. She also had the wrong personality for the job and lacked the grit and determination that is required. A good firefighter is often described as being 'switched on', or 'all about', whereas the best way to describe her would have been 'switched off' and 'all over the place'. I remember one night shift when we picked up a job on our little one appliance stations ground. It wasn't much of a job, but still required the use of BA. As we got up from our seats to go to the appliance, she was heard to say something but it was inaudible over the noise of the bells. When we got on the appliance and pulled out of the bay, I asked her what it was she had said. "I was asking if anyone had turned the oven off." she said. The other firefighter on the back and I both looked at her and said, "No, we didn't even know the oven was on?" She said, "I put a pie in there for my dinner." My mate turned and said, "But you ran straight past the oven on the way to the bay. Why didn't you turn it off then?" I didn't understand her mumbled reply, but her mind must have been somewhere else because when we arrived at the address, she dismounted the machine with her tunic, helmet, gloves and BA set on, but no boots and leggings! She was supposed to be my BA partner and be entering the house with me. I had to enter the building alone with the hosereel while my mate, after already opening the door with a sledgehammer, hurriedly pulled a set on before joining me inside. Luckily, it wasn't much of a job and it went out quickly. While we were in there, as it wasn't far from the station, our governor told her to walk back to the station and turn the oven out before someone else gets a fire call to smoke issuing from our station. Once everything was damped down, we dumped our sets back on the machine and started to make the hose and gear up. It took a while to get everything stowed and the tank topped up, but there still was no sign of her. The governor started to get concerned that something had happened to her, as it shouldn't have taken her that long to walk to the station and back. As we went to mount the appliance to go looking for her, we found her hiding around the other side of the pump ladder, eating her pie! In total contrast, the other female firefighter that I served with on that watch, at the same time, was one of the best firefighters that I ever served with. She was so switched on that she would often be a step in front of everyone else. Her brain was as sharp as a razor blade, as was her whit. She oozed common sense and never shied away from anything. Her ability as a brigade driver was also impressive. One night, before she joined my watch, she was driving her crew to a shout when the appliance brakes failed as she was approaching a busy T - junction with traffic lights. Instead of panicking, she worked out what her options were and picked a spot to aim the machine at, which was a small service road on the other side of the junction. Everything happened so quickly that the crew didn't realise what was happening until they had come to a safe halt. The consequences could have been disastrous, but no one was injured. Afterwards, she said she chose the service road because there was a metal barrier across it a little way down and it would be better if she used that to halt them, rather than another car. Now that is quick thinking! I worked with her on several jobs and always felt happy and secure to do so. I think she would have made a good officer because she had all the right attributes – more so than a lot of male officers. Her sense of humour was perfect for life on a fire station, too. All in all, she was a pleasure to work with and a good firefighter.

Another time I saw two extremes was at a job that we picked up just before knocking off time on a day shift. I was riding the back of the pump ladder and designated BA wearer, along with the firefighter that I described earlier. It was a fire in a house and was going quite well in one of the upstairs bedrooms. I entered first and she followed me, but I had to pull the hosereel in with me, which is usually the job of the number two in the crew. She just followed me around and didn't do very much at all. The room on fire was put out pretty quickly and I set about searching the other rooms for possible casualties. It was common practice, in a small building like a house, for the two BA wearers to split up and search the property between them. However, I had spectator with me, so I had to search all the rooms more or less on my own. I noticed that the ceiling had partly collapsed and the fire had got into the roof space above us. Once a fire gets in the roof, it's very difficult to bring back under control. I got on my radio and asked for a short extension ladder and a ceiling hook to be brought to the front door, then I told my BA partner to go down and bring them up while I was doing my best to hit the fire where I could. She was gone for ages and I was having limited success, so I went down the stairs to see what the hold up was. I saw the ladder and ceiling hook, so I carried them up the stairs and started to attack the fire through the loft hatch. Suddenly, I felt very sick. I thought I was going to throw up in my mask and my legs felt like jelly. I knew something was wrong with me so, reluctantly, I put the hosereel down and started to make my way out; still no sign of my partner. As I went down the stairs, I was passed by another BA crew going up. They were from my old watch on my previous station who had been mobilised because of the multiple calls being received and the fact that my useless OIC at the time had panicked on arrival and made pumps four. I staggered outside to shut down and dump my set, but knew I wasn't going to make it back to the appliance. I dropped to my knees behind the machine and removed my facemask and helmet, then undid the straps of the set and opened my tunic. I was just trying to cool my body, having recognises the early signs of heat exhaustion. I'd over done it inside, trying to do it all by myself because I had no one helping me. I was on my hands and knees, gulping air into my lungs, but I didn't have the energy to do anything else. No one had noticed that I was struggling, but then another appliance turned up from a neighbouring station as part of the make up. The female junior officer in charge of that appliance, who I knew and liked, came straight over to me; even before reporting to the OIC of the job. "OK, Steve? You're struggling mate. Here, let me give you a hand." She lifted the set from my back and took my tunic off. My T-shirt underneath was saturated with sweat. She helped me to my feet and escorted me to our pump ladder, where she sat me down and gave me some water to drink. She stayed with me until I said I was feeling better. To me, that is the mark of a good firefighter. The ability to recognise what is most important at any given moment and prioritising accordingly; also, looking out for your mates. I've never forgotten that. When I'd recovered enough, I went round the back to speak to my old watch and see how things were going and if they needed anything. Then, I went and found my OIC, who was standing well away from operations, abiding by the theory book on being an officer. I relayed the valuable information that I had gathered for him, but was totally ignored. He seemed to be in some sort of trance and detached from what was going on in front of him. I lost interest at that pint and set about looking for my BA partner, so I could find out what had happened to her. I found her sitting in a car with a woman, a few house down from the job. I knocked on the window and asked what she was doing. "This lady is pregnant and was stressed about the fire, so I thought I'd come and sit with her to reassure her." She obviously didn't see her role in the brigade in the same way that I saw mine.

So, there you have it. There isn't a definitive answer as to whether women can be firefighters. Clearly, some can, as I have found out from experience, but others shouldn't even think about it. But is it their fault when they are faced with a job that they really don't want to do, or aren't capable of doing? I don't think so. I blame politicians and the pressure they put on fire services to recruit those who tick their diversity boxes. I want to make perfectly clear that I came across many male firefighters who have been totally useless, over the years. Usually, those who were targeted and persuaded that a career in the fire brigade was for them. Like I said at the start, it's a very controversial subject, but not one that I feel I needed to avoid. I've given my views based on my own personal experiences. Someone else's views and experiences might be different, but I take as I find and have never glossed over anything to please or appease.

PROLOGUE

There won't be any more books on the Fire Service from me, even though I've just scratched the surface in the two that I've now written. There is so much more to tell, but that's a job for someone else now. Even though many people will hate some of what I've written, (my style might be a bit too straight and blunt), but I hope that the majority who have read it will have enjoyed this deeply personal account of events as I saw and still see them. The aim of my writing has always been to inform and entertain the reader. I've never strayed from the truth as I saw it just to please people. I hope others who decide to write on the subject adopt the same ethos. Otherwise, what's the point?

ABOUT THE AUTHOR

Stephen Charles

The two books that Steve has written, give an idea of what it was like to spend a prolonged period of time serving as a front line Firefighter in the London Fire Brigade. Steve is now retired and living in rural Suffolk with his two greyhounds and, now that a few of the ghosts have been layed to rest, he plans on writing his first novel.

BOOKS BY THIS AUTHOR

Blood, Soot And Tears

A hard hitting and brutally honest account of life as a frontline firefighter in the London Fire Brigade, from initial application to retirement and beyond. It cover a 25 year career and no punches are pulled. Training, station life, incidents, politics and mental heaqlth are all laid open with modest honesty.